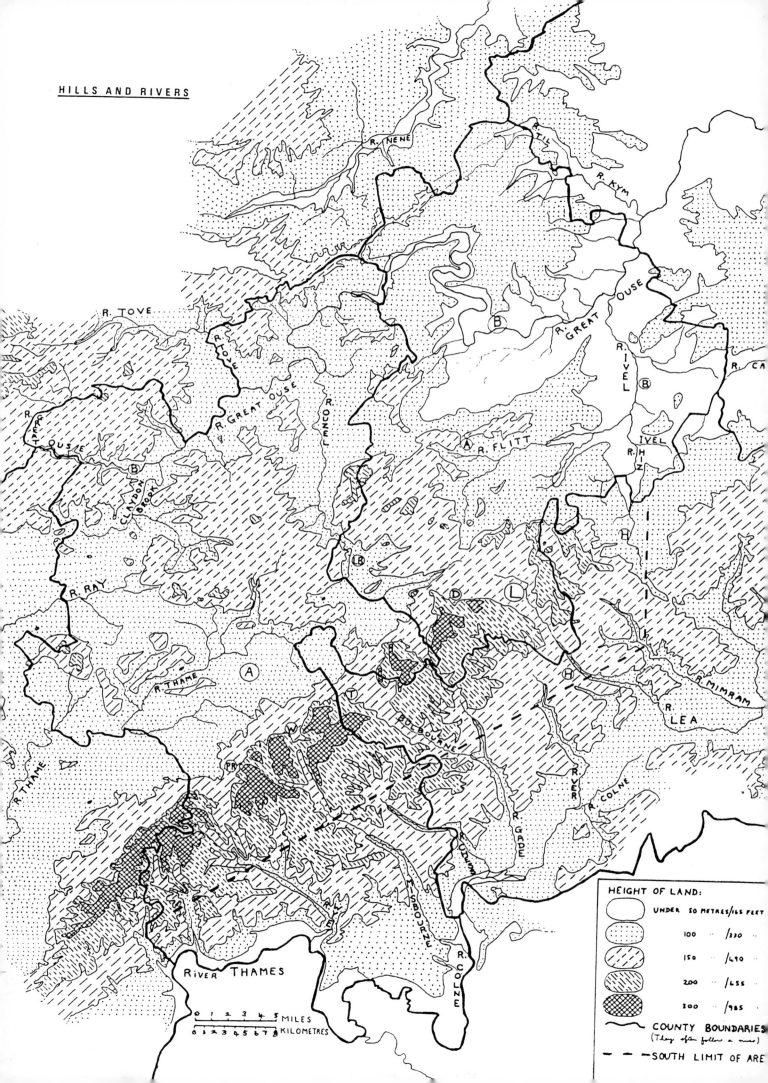

HILLS AND RIVERS

R. NENE

R. TIL

R. KYM

R. TOVE

R. TOVE

R. GREAT OUSE

R. OUZEL

A R. FLITT

R. GREAT OUSE

R. GREAT OUSE

CLAYDON BROOK

R. RAY

R. THAME

R. THAME

R. THAME

River THAMES

R. GREAT OUSE

B

R. MIMRAM

R. LEA

R. COLNE

R. COLNE

RIVER GADE

R. MISBOURNE

A

T

W

PR

BULBOURNE

B

D

L

H

H

A

B

B

R. IVEL

IVEL

R. HIZ

R. CA

0 1 2 3 4 5 MILES
0 1 2 3 4 5 6 7 8 KILOMETRES

TOWNS AND VILLAGES
portrayed or mentioned

NORTHAMPTONSHIRE

CAMBRIDGESHIRE

BEDFORDSHIRE

Dean
Melchbourne   Swineshead
Podington
Souldrop   Riseley   Keysoe
Hinwick
Bushmead
Sharnbrook
Colmworth
Odell   Thurleigh
Felmersham
Harrold
Chellington   Pavenham
Lavendon   Carlton   Oakley
Turvey   Stevington
Renhold
OLNEY   Great
Ravenstone   Newton   Bromham   Barford
Blossomville   Stagsden   **BEDFORD**   Everton
Emberton   Biddenham   Willington
Great   Cople   **SANDY**   Potton
Hanslope   Tyringham   Sherington   **KEMPSTON**   Cardington
Gayhurst   Lathbury   Chicheley   Elstow   Northill   Eyeworth
North   Stewartby   Old   Dunton
NEWPORT   Crawley   Marston   Houghton   Warden
Great   **PAGNELL**   Cranfield   Moretaine   Conquest   Haynes   Southill   **BIGGLESWADE**
WOLVERTON   Linford   Willen   Millbrook   Chicksands
Moulsoe   Marston   Maulden   Shefford
STONY   **MILTON**   Milton   **AMPTHILL**   Clophill   Meppershall
STRATFORD   **KEYNES**   Keynes   Flitton   Silsoe   Shillington
Stowe   Steppingley   **FLITWICK**   Pulloxhill
Aspley   Westoning   **HITCHIN**
Maids   Guise   Eversholt   Barton
Moreton   **BLETCHLEY**   Bow   Husborne   Milton   Harlington   Pirton
BUCKINGHAM   Brickhill   Crawley   Bryan   Sharpenhoe   Preston
Thornborough   Whaddon Chase   Woburn   Toddington   Sundon   Kings
Heath   Streatley   Walden
Hillesden   **WINSLOW**   & Reach   **HOUGHTON**   Lilley
Swanbourne   **REGIS**   Whitwell
Steeple   Middle   **LEIGHTON**   **LUTON**
Claydon   Claydon   Stewkley   **LINSLADE**   Kimpton
East   Soulbury   Tilsworth
Marsh   Claydon   Creslow   Eaton   Totternhoe
Gibbon   Oving   Whitchurch   Wing   Bray   **DUNSTABLE**   **HARPENDEN**
Quainton   Pitchcott   Mentmore   Slapton   Whipsnade   Caddington
Waddesdon   Edlesborough   Hyde
Wotton   Hulcott   Ivinghoe
Underwood   **AYLESBURY**   Bierton   Pitstone   **HARPENDEN**
Boarstall   Brill   Marsworth   Aldbury
Lower   Weston   **TRING**   Little   Great
Oakley   Chilton   Winchendon   Turville   Gaddesden   Gaddesden
Chearsley   Dinton   Halton   **BERKHAMSTED**
Ickford   Long   **HADDENHAM**   Ellesborough   **WENDOVER**   **HEMEL**
Crendon   Cholesbury   **HEMPSTEAD**
PRINCES   Dunsmore
RISBOROUGH   Great   Little
Bledlow   Hampden   Hampden
Lacey   **CHESHAM**
Radnage   Green
Bradenham
West
OXFORDSHIRE   Ibstone   Wycombe
Turville
Fingest   **HIGH WYCOMBE**

BUCKINGHAMSHIRE

HERTFORDSHIRE

0 1 2 3 4 5 MILES
0 1 2 3 4 5 6 7 8 KILOMETRES

BERKSHIRE

GREATER LONDON

CHANGES IN OUR LANDSCAPE

Aspects of Bedfordshire,
Buckinghamshire and
the Chilterns

1947 – 1992

from
the photographic work

of
Eric G. Meadows

To Muriel

KEYSOE, Bedfordshire. A timber-framed cottage in Keysoe Row East being re-thatched with straw by Evans of Riseley.
20 Jan. 1986

The completed roof on 'The Homestead', Keysoe Row East.
12 June 1986

First published October 1992
by
The Book Castle
12 Church Street
Dunstable
Bedfordshire LU5 4RU

ISBN 1 871199 31 X

Computer Typeset by 'Globetype',
Luton, Bedfordshire.
Printed and bound by Hartnolls Ltd,
Bodmin, Cornwall.

CONTENTS

Our area is the whole of Bedfordshire with most of Buckinghamshire plus north-west Hertfordshire to about 8 miles south of the Chiltern scarp.

ABBREVIATIONS USED IN THE CAPTIONS:

BBONT	= Berkshire, Buckinghamshire & Oxford-shire Naturalists' Trust Ltd.	I.B.A	= Institute of British Architects
c.	= *circa*, about	Local N.R.	= nature reserve of the Wildlife Trust of Bedfordshire & Cambridgeshire
C	= century		
C.C.	= County Council	N.N.R.	= National Nature Reserve
C.P.	= Country Park (set up by the County Council)	N.T.	= National Trust property
		R.C.	= Roman Catholic
d.	= died	Y.H.A.	= Youth Hostels' Association
E.H.	= English Heritage		

ACKNOWLEDGEMENTS

Many people have helped me in the course of my photographic work. For allowing me on their land to photograph their property I wish to thank:

The Administrator, Waddesdon Manor

Ashridge Management College

Mrs. P. Brunner, Wotton House

Berkshire, Buckinghamshire & Oxfordshire Naturalists' Trust

Buckinghamshire Railway Centre

English Heritage

The National Trust

Owners of gardens open under the National Gardens Scheme

Bedfordshire County Council

Luton Hoo Estate

Mrs. Orlebar of Hinwick House

The R.A.F. and U.S.A.F. at Chicksands

Shuttleworth College of Agriculture

The Shuttleworth Collection

Many farmers, including Mr. R. T. Franklin, Pegsdon Common Farm

St. Albans Photoprint aided me with the maps, and Dr. Anne Brenchley (English Nature) gave advice.

I am particularly grateful to Eric Brandreth (Harpenden Librarian), Betty Chambers (editor of the *Bedfordshire Magazine*), James Dyer, F.S.A. and David Henden for reading the manuscript and making many helpful suggestions. I am also most grateful to James Dyer for writing the Foreword.

I thank my wife, Muriel, for proof reading and for her patient support during the two years of the book's preparation.

Finally I thank Paul Bowes of the Book Castle for his expertise and on-going encouragement, assisted by commercial artist Trevor Wood, to make my material into this book.

Eric Meadows
Harpenden, 1992

PODINGTON, Bedfordshire. Hinwick House built of stone 1709-14 for Richard Orlebar, who was probably the architect. He was a huntsman and his wife was Diana, hence the pediment sculpture of goddess Diana the huntress. The Orlebar family lived here until 1992 when the house was put on the market (see p.165).　　*28 Aug. 1974*

FOREWORD

ALTHOUGH he experimented with a simple camera when a boy, Eric Meadows' photographic career really began after the War, when films, temporarily unavailable, once more became readily accessible. Eric's pictures were not created on a whim with a mere press of the shutter-release button. Each was carefully planned and created, often taking up to an hour to compose, after days of waiting for the right weather, light and time of day. The result has been this outstanding record, collected over nearly half a century, of the changing scene in a part of England that is too readily overlooked. Many of the pictures portray little-known corners of Bedfordshire, Buckinghamshire and north-west Hertfordshire, recording the changes that our violent century has wrought on the rural landscape, urban townscape and social scene.

The Eric Meadows collection of photographs will be a source of constant reference for future generations of researchers, seeking to find the essence of our area in the second half of the 20th century. They will join with us in thanking him for producing such a faithful record of a transient period in our nation's history.

James Dyer

HARLINGTON, Bedfordshire. Looking down on East End Farm and English elms in the gault vale. Sharpenhoe Clappers (N.T.), crowned by a beech grove, had grassy steeps still mainly free of hawthorn scrub. Beyond Sharpenhoe (left) are the Barton Hills (see p.105 & 109). *25 April 1954*

OLD WARDEN, Bedfordshire. Like a glimpse of an earlier age, here is an evocative fragment of a great house built of brick c.1545. It is on the Warden Abbey site acquired by the Gostwick family of Willington. Most of it was demolished in 1790. In 1975 the Landmark Trust restored this remnant with a stepped gable below its fine chimney stack, seen with pear blossom. Nearby are hollows which were monastic fishponds, also a mid 16C barn with diapered brick walls.   *1 April 1990*

INTRODUCTION

The landscape of our area is determined by its foundations, bands of rock-strata extending south-west to north-east. The oldest rocks are in the north, oolitic limestones exposed by the Great Ouse as it cuts through the Oxford clay. Limestones of the Portland and Purbeck series also cap low hills north of and in the Vale of Aylesbury, which is of Kimmeridge clay drained by the river Thame. Lower greensand forms the height on which the Buckinghamshire Brickhill (meaning 'hilltop') villages stand, and it extends eastwards as a ridge across Bedfordshire. Southwards is the Chiltern downland, three beds of chalk with a gault plain along its north foot. The chalk was rounded, broken into promontories and cut into steep-sided valleys, some with streams flowing south, by ice sheets that deposited clays and gravels on the chalk plateau. The ice sheets also blanketed the lower land with boulder clay and left deposits of sand and gravel.

This geology gives great diversity of soils and it provided the traditional building materials – stone for walls in the north reminiscent of the Cotswolds, rust-stained sandstone dug out of the greensand, flint and Totternhoe stone or clunch in the south; also from the late 15th century local-made bricks and tiles of different rich colours from the clays and brick-earths. Timber framing with wattle-and-daub infill was used for cottages where other materials were not to hand, thatched with straw or reeds. Brick was used increasingly from mid 18th century, in Georgian buildings in more elaborate ways such as different coloured headers. The Victorians introduced distinct varieties of stone and Welsh slate, brought in by canals and railways.

Bedfordshire has always had much arable ground, its heavy clays good for growing corn and the lighter soils for market gardening; but in mid and north Buckinghamshire there is (or was before 1980) a preponderance of pasture. Enclosure from common fields was late, mainly in 18-19th century by Parliamentary Commissioners, giving many straight hawthorn and blackthorn hedges, straight lengths of road, isolated farms with their houses, and a few fairly large woods. Where hedges are sinuous and of mixed species with fields small and irregular, enclosure was earlier – 14-17th century. In contrast the Chilterns have always been well wooded, little irregular fields with old hedges around them, numerous small woods, ponds in pastures, woods or rough grazing for sheep on the steep slopes and downs. The few meadows were near the villages centred on streams in the valleys, with winding lanes and many paths to hamlets.

Following the Reformation wealthy families settled in this countryside, building houses with gardens in small parks. During the 17th and 18th centuries they often had them enlarged and altered in contemporary styles by architects and gardeners – expression of their wealth and status. Most famous are the English landscape gardens at Stowe near Buckingham and the similar gardens at West Wycombe. Other mansions and parks are at Ashridge, Luton Hoo and along the greensand ridge at Woburn, Ampthill, Silsoe, Southill, Old Warden and Sandy. In the 19th century the Rothschild family liked the Vale of Aylesbury countryside so much that six members built mansions in gardens and parks there.

Ancient roads cross our countryside, the prehistoric track called the Icknield Way follows the north scarp of the Chilterns, and the Roman Watling Street and Akeman Street run northwards from London. These roads were turnpiked in 17-18th century for stage coaches. Waterways for merchandise were the Ouse Navigation up to Bedford by 1689, followed by the Ivel Navigation to Biggleswade in 1758 and to Shefford in 1822. The Grand Junction Canal from the Thames to the Midlands through Hertfordshire and Buckinghamshire was fully opened in 1811, with a branch to Aylesbury in 1815. The waterways became less used as railways were built – the line to Birmingham from Euston was opened in 1837-8, with branches to Aylesbury 1839, Bedford 1846 and Dunstable 1848. The Great Northern from Kings Cross came through Biggleswade and Sandy in 1850. However the main railways and roads had little impact on our countryside as they crossed it from London to the industrial north, other than development of market gardening after the Great Northern came.

It can be seen that our landscape is very varied but almost wholly shaped by man. At the turn of this century it was all but rural – Luton with the hat trade was its largest town with 36,404 people, Bedford with schools and agricultural engineering had 35,144, while the largest town in Buckinghamshire was furniture-making High Wycombe with 19,282 people. Aylesbury had 9,240, Hemel Hempstead 11,264 and Hitchin 10,072 residents. The total population of our area was about 348,000. The railway network was complete, so that few places were more than about seven miles from a station. Carriers' horse-drawn vehicles conveyed goods and people to and from the villages – closely-knit communities and mainly self-sufficient – from which most people travelled little, except for occasional visits to their nearest market town. Much was to change during the next century.

Early in the 20th century electrical and diesel power allowed industry to be sited away from coalfields. Cheap electricity, availability of land and ample labour soon brought motor vehicle, engineering, electrical and chemical works to Luton. Agricultural depression (from 1873), except during the two world wars, caused a drift of workers from the land. By the 1920s carriers' carts were displaced by motor buses which, with trains, gave easier access to the larger towns. Only the more affluent minority had cars. Country folk could see the higher living standards in the towns, new houses and a chance of work in new industries. Some left their villages but, as bus services improved, others went daily to work in the towns. However a number of rural district councils built council houses, so that for a low rent farmworkers could remain in their villages. The General Slump in the 1930s brought workers from other parts of Britain. Towns grew, with rows of terraced or semi-detached houses and often ribbon development along the main roads. Luton and neighbouring Dunstable more than trebled their population in the half century, Aylesbury and Hemel Hempstead more than doubled; but Bedford, Hitchin and some smaller places only increased by a half. The increase for our whole area was around three-quarters to about 600,000. Much land was left as rough pasture or scrub woodland in mid and north Buckinghamshire where population declined, but in south Buckinghamshire 'Metroland' numbers of people increased considerably with much building. Shepherding on the downs ceased about 1930 and in 1940 intensive farming began. Coppicing is a way of obtaining a greater quantity of wood in a few years at very much less cost than trees for timber; in decline for decades, it virtually ceased, as did pollarding of riverside willows. The many little brickyards were superseded by large Fletton works with clusters of chimneys sited on the Oxford clay, the one renamed Stewartby, south-west of Bedford, claiming in 1936 to be the largest brickworks in the world. There were lime and cement works on the chalk, sandpits in the greensand, and for war-time airfield runways gravel digging made lakes in the Ouse valley.

Since 1945 our countryside – an intact living record of hundreds of years – has been ravaged by heavily-subsidised agriculture. Farmers have been forced by government policies to cultivate almost every usable bit of land, so many ancient as well as Enclosure Act hedgerows including their trees were grubbed out, old woods cleared and marshes drained. Footpaths, that are statutory rights of way, are repeatedly ploughed up (but by law should be reinstated within 14 days and kept clear); also paths have often been obstructed or possibly dangerous animals used to deter walkers. Despite this, following footpaths and bridleways is the best way to see the countryside. Modern ploughs that go deeper have damaged and sometimes destroyed barrows, earthworks and sites of deserted villages. Farming employs far fewer people due to mechanisation and the routine of spraying. Most farmed land has been ploughed; if grassland for mowing or grazing, sown with specially-developed high-yielding grasses and sprayed with weedkillers. Nearly two-thirds is under cereals (with barley leading); they and a few other crops are sprayed also with insecticides and sometimes fungicides, and high rates of artificial fertilisers are applied. New barns are often obtrusive and unsightly. Poultry, calves and pigs are kept in battery units with feed – the main purpose of the tillage – provided. Quantity, not necessarily human nutritional quality, has been the aim. Except for a few big farmers the main beneficiaries of this 'maximum production from the land at any cost' are agribusiness and the moneylenders. These agricultural methods, with less mixed farming, have brought a dull uniformity and some ugliness to much of our rural landscape.

From 1950 the villages and towns in our countryside have had to accept many more people, including resettlement of London overspill, and the New Towns of Hemel Hempstead from 1947 and Milton Keynes from 1967. Town and Country Planning has controlled uses of land and regulated building, also areas in and near towns and large villages are made zones for industry and commerce. The Chilterns have been designated an Area of Outstanding Natural Beauty, there is a Green Belt in the south, and parts of towns and villages with character have been made Conservation Areas. As car ownership increased from mid 1950s and even more in 1965-90, so railway branches were closed. Main lines were improved, using diesel engines until electrification. Bus services too declined very much, limited eventually to a poor service where there is sufficient demand. Because of car mobility many people commute into towns and cities for their work but live in smaller towns, villages and sometimes in open country. Most villages have been infilled or had estates of indifferent urban housing added to them, completely changing their character. Commuters, retired people and developers buy old cottages and cottage rows, alter, combine and sometimes extend them. Prices are too high for country people. If they cannot find a council house (built in mid century) that is still for rent, farmworkers may be forced to move into poorer houses in towns. The population of our area has doubled in 40 years to about 1,200,000. County councils are obliged by government to plan for the estimated increase in population for each decade ahead. To

LUTON. In 1901 a municipal electricity works was opened beside the medieval vicarage, to supply the cheapest DC electricity in the country (at a cost in grime and drizzle!). Before 1930 it supplied an area westwards as far as Wing. From Crescent Road over railway sidings, this is the enlarged works starting up at dusk and offending the Clean Air Act 1956. It was demolished in 1971-2. *19 Nov. 1956*

their credit, planners and private estates together have done (and continue to do) a wonderful job in containing this explosion of urban development in a traditional rural area.

The impact of these changes on the landscape and wildlife is enormous – houses, factories, water supplies, electricity pylons, airfields, motorways, bypasses and other road improvements. Traffic is greatly increased on all roads, with giant container lorries and vibration from heavy vehicles. Pressure too is exerted by many feet on paths and vegetation in popular places, with litter and some wilful damage. Leisure activities have increased but space is limited, as it is for habitats of mammals, birds, insects and plants of which the losses are tremendous. Very little flower-rich grassland remains, and that only in paddocks, on road verges, on uncultivated slopes of the downs and greensand ridge, and in parks. Many of these plant-rich sites are nature reserves of English Nature or wildlife trusts, are on National Trust land or in country parks set up by the county councils; in all of them old practices of grazing or cutting of the vegetation have been restored. Before myxomatosis in 1953, rabbits controlled hawthorn and briar scrub, which now must be cleared occasionally by conservators. Woods are small in extent and usually private, but there is much woodland on National Trust land especially at Ashridge. Forest is planted on the larger landed estates, and more by the Forestry Commission which has nature trails in its woods. Rivers have often been dredged and straightened, partly treated as channels for street drainage and effluent. Flooded clay and gravel pits are now used for water-sports or as nature reserves, and the county councils propose to plant many trees where the land is bare.

About 1970 two sites were threatened with development as London's third airport. A little later came a great loss, the tall and distinctive English elms were killed by Dutch elm disease; but if allowed their suckers can grow into new trees. Tidying by farmers – overlopping hedges, pottering

with weedkillers or clearing tangled corners – often destroys what is unusual, has beauty and meaning. Planting trees and grass makes scenery, not landscape which needs the human element. Replanting of hedgerows and woods is a very poor substitute for what has been destroyed. Any remains of the original must be cherished (like a work of art or historic building) and where possible encouraged to return, such as trees allowed to grow from existing saplings or suckers rather than by planting. Planting the wrong tree species urbanises and spoils as much as bad buildings. English Nature designates Sites of Special Scientific Interest by notifying owners and occupiers of the interest on their land, but despite penalties too many are lost; by accidental damage (such as leaching of nitrates and spray drift), by planning decisions (such as new roads), and by lack of management. Farmers still receive subsidies for over-production, but can now receive payments for set-aside. These can be enhanced in Bedfordshire and Hertfordshire by the Countryside Commission's Premium Scheme, which gives extra monies when set-aside land is managed for people, wildlife and landscape; English Nature gives its own advice on this. The Commission's Countryside Stewardship scheme goes further – 10-year agreements, with annual payments for restoration and management of chalk grassland, lowland heath and wetlands. It is to be hoped that all farmers will soon considerably improve the landscape value of the land they use.

The following reproductions from my photographs taken during the past 46 years show some of the best, unusual or unique features of this landscape, some things considerably changed, others unchanged, some as they are now and a few of things that have gone. Many are in the same parishes, but such a cluster is necessary to give an adequate picture of the place. All the captions end with the date when the photograph was taken.

I hope my illustrations will convey the beauty and the individuality in this landscape, and give pleasure to many people.

MELCHBOURNE, Bedfordshire. In this little village The Street faces Melchbourne Park (private apartments), beyond the church mostly rebuilt in 1779. The Street was a row of 16 simple thatched cottages (only half visible here), looking most impressive with repetition. The St. John family built them in the first half of the 18C, so they are an early example of estate dwellings of high quality. Unfortunately the northern half was demolished after a fire in 1961. *20 April 1958*

MY LANDSCAPE PHOTOGRAPHY

The challenge faced by a landscape photographer is to make part of the three dimensional original with movement, life and colour into at least a pleasing one-plane reproduction that holds attention; if possible it should be a picture in which arrangement of the subject matter and the proportions are both in balance and a joy to many viewers. It should have a touch of glory, also often convey the atmosphere or mood of a place.

Unlike the person who draws or paints, the photographer is limited by the photographic system; for instance, unwanted objects or features cannot be moved if they are big and fixed, also can only be removed from monochrome negatives or prints with difficulty and not at all from transparencies. Perspective can only be varied by employing different lenses – wide angle in restricted space and for foreground prominence, long focus for a distant view of part of a scene. Viewpoint is all-important and often crucial, to take in what is wanted but to exclude what is not required.

Coupled with choice of viewpoint is the equally essential one of lighting. One has to use available light, using the sun as a spot or floodlight in addition to general skylight. Contrast needs to be within limits; for example, without sunlight or with the sun dead behind one the contrast may be too low, giving a soft, flat or dull result especially in monochrome (but see Woburn countryside on page 134). Looking into the sun can give too high a contrast, also light scatter in the lens (despite its coating) may cause unwanted patterns and patches of light. The eye can accommodate a much higher contrast range than film. With monochrome film the latitude of exposure is much greater than with colour film; also contrast corrections can be made during print making, by choice of contrast grade of paper and by 'shading' (varying exposure of parts of the print). With monochrome one needs to know the approximate tone that colours will give, for instance, water among grass under a blue sky may be invisible as water takes on the colour of the sky; there has to be contrast in tones. A medium yellow glass filter over the lens is usual with monochrome film to separate tones of blue sky and clouds. Cloud patterns and formations often make an ideal background. Also important is the variety of light and shade given by sunlight and cloud shadows. Photographs generally need either a light or a dark foreground to suggest depth. Glancing or side lighting is essential to show texture, especially important in monochrome.

Due to changes in altitude and angle of the sun, there is an ideal time of day and time of year for the right lighting on particular subjects. In some cases it may be limited to a few minutes, but often must be within an hour or two according to how one is approaching the subject. In summer, midday sunlight is not good for landscapes in this locality as shadows are likely to be too small; 2-3 hours after sunrise and 2-3 hours before sunset are usually much better, when low angle of lighting shows folds or hollows in the ground. Haze can be a big problem, reducing contrast and causing over-blueness; it is often worse in summer and perhaps later in the day, but can occur at any time in our polluted atmosphere. Trees too are dense, solid-looking and dark green in mid to late summer. Tracery of bare trees can be fascinating. The ideal times are probably as the deciduous leaves come and go. November is often my most rewarding month.

What to photograph and how to do it is an individual and personal choice, just as is the choice of equipment. Most of my monochrome photographs have been taken with reflex cameras, except for a few interiors on larger sheet film. One camera is a single lens reflex that allows the lens to be changed for wide angle, long focus or telephoto; but these lenses are all heavy and the finder image disappears at the moment of film exposure. My favourite is the old and now obsolete Rolleiflex with twin lenses that cannot be changed. It is lightweight and has a large clear viewfinder, so that it can even be used upside down over my head to give a higher viewpoint. This makes the foreground more distant, rises above obstructions such as hedges and walls; also slightly reduces convergence of verticals in buildings. A chest-high viewpoint is often too low on level ground, and more so if the ground rises ahead. I use fast roll film processed in a fine grain developer to give the contrast and quality of negative required for the enlarged print. The 2¼ inch or 56 millimetre square negative is large enough for all or part of it to make a good print of any shape, the pictorial proportions being decided when the enlarged print is made. Editors of magazines and books sometimes use only a part of my print, which can spoil the proportions I have chosen. In this book the choice has been mine.

The colour illustrations are all from my 5×4 inch transparencies. These are made with a large folding view-camera set on a tripod. Lenses of different focal lengths are used, each mounted in a shutter. I compose the picture upside down on ground-glass, beneath an opaque cloth as Victorian photographers used to do. This is necessary with this size to obtain the required definition (sharpness) in all parts. It entails the focusing of different parts of the image individually, viewed through an 8-times magnifier, by using the camera's movements – swinging and tilting back and/or front (lens). Sheet colour film in a light-proof holder is then put in place of the ground-glass and the calculated exposure made. Exposure time with colour film is critical (technically to ⅓ of a 'stop' or 'f' number with a fixed speed of shutter), calculated with an electronic flash meter. Alterations in colour processing time can be used to correct exposure, but it slightly changes colour balance and contrast so has to be judged carefully. All this work involves carrying 20-23lbs./9-10kg. of equipment, and many subjects I find or like are some distance from roads. The 5×4 inch transparency is the smallest original accepted by many printers of large reproductions for posters and calendars.

With colour film one has to think of colours in the subject, one needs to compose or balance them. Blue and green alone can be dull or monotonous. Also colour of the light varies: it can be too yellow early and late in the day, but at any time in the middle of the day there may be over-blueness from the sky, from haze, or both. It is corrected by judged use of pale yellow gelatine filters, shielded from sunlight and placed before the lens. High contrast of lighting and large areas of deep shadow have to be avoided; also printers do not like grey in the sky. The illustrations of Carlton on pages 119 and 161 show the difference of approach for colour and monochrome.

The photographer has to respect private land and ask permission to go on it. However, problems arise: once two C.I.D. officers called on me after I had been seen by my car in a lane, on the bank to take photographs of a Georgian house behind a brick wall. The owners feared I was 'casing' their property!

A photographer needs to know the landscape well, local weather and its likely variations (watched continually), much of natural history, architecture and local history. One has to have particular subjects in mind or noted, find viewpoints for them that meet most of the requirements, then return to them perhaps several times when weather, lighting and other factors may be suitable (often they are not). Pleasing foregrounds can be difficult to find. Many wild flowers are too small and can only be used in a mass; also they are very much less abundant now. Windswept vegetation, ripples or waves on water and swirls in clouds suggest movement. People if not too prominent, animals, buildings, berries or fruits as well as flowers give scale and added interest. A photographer must sometimes act very quickly to catch a fleeting variation in the subject or its lighting; at other times be prepared to wait for several hours for the right lighting or clouds. The 5×4 camera may have to be covered with a plastic bag when a shower comes, and re-focused again if it is blown over. Finally, despite all the photographer's skills, high aims and continual strivings, luck is always welcome.

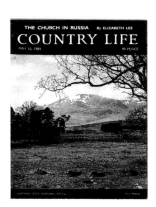

When leaving the army after the war I could not find photographic work to my liking, so continued in clerical employment. My demob. leave in September and October 1947 gave me my first sight of Scotland – seven glorious weeks never to be forgotten. The photographs taken then during four weeks on Skye, with more during a fortnight's holiday in 1948 and in 1949, were enough for *The Skye Scene* (Oliver & Boyd, 1951), a book with over 70 monochrome plates, long out of print. My local photography was restricted to Saturday afternoons, Sundays and summer evenings, by cycling until 1954, by moped or scooter until 1965. Photographs of churches, monuments and mansions in Buckinghamshire, Northamptonshire, Bedfordshire and Huntingdonshire were taken for Pevsner's *Buildings of England*. Over 100 photographs illustrated the 1962 and 1975 editions of the *Pictorial Guide to Bedfordshire,* and others for Joyce Godber's *History of Bedfordshire*. Redundancy in 1973 allowed me to work at photography full time. This gave me the chance to write in 1976 the *Pictorial Guide to Hertfordshire* with 118 illustrations, companion to the Bedfordshire volume; also, in 1985, *Luton Parish Church* with 42 illustrations (available only at the church). Many photographs have appeared in the *Bedfordshire Magazine*. In 46 years a collection of over 21,000 monochrome negatives (with complete records) has been assembled, of which those in this book are a selection.

Colour photographs were taken as 35mm. transparencies from 1951, and in 1966 work began with 5×4 inch sheet film. From 1973 this was pursued further and is now my main work. About 20 of my colour photographs have made covers for *Country Life,* some for *The Field,* and in other magazines like *This England* and *Evergreen,* but a greater number have been and are used in calendars including trade publications. Scotland, especially the Highlands and all its western isles, is still an abiding love, so in May and October much of my work is done there.

Eric Meadows

BUCKINGHAMSHIRE

OLNEY.
Georgian houses of local grey stone, like many lining the long unbroken High Street that is wide for the market. The early 14C church steeple is the only medieval spire in the county.   *July 1978*
◄

OLNEY.
The early 19C mill, miller's house and church from the broad water-meadows grazed by cows with horns. The mill was demolished c.1966 after a fire (see p.57).
▼   *June 1959*

NORTH BUCKINGHAMSHIRE

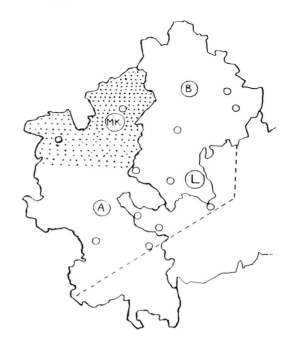

This is mostly a countryside of gentle undulations, fields with hedges and hedgerow trees, many lanes and paths, and a few woods. Sometimes there are longer views, as northwards from Whaddon Chase and the Brickhill villages. Much of the Great Ouse and its tributary river Tove are the boundary with Northamptonshire, the county of stone spires which has given us the fine ones at Hanslope and Olney. Oolitic limestone was used for noble churches at Hillesden and Maids Moreton, also for the mansions at Gayhurst and Claydon. There is good townscape: of stone in Olney, of stone and brick in Stony Stratford, Buckingham and Winslow.

Wealthy Georgians had a passion for grand houses and gardens. At Stowe, Sir Richard Temple (later Lord Cobham) inherited in 1697 a modest brick house with formal enclosed gardens. He, influenced and assisted by Vanburgh (who enlarged the house) and from 1713-25 by Charles Bridgeman, surveyor and gardener, made larger gardens. Behind a ha-ha they were open to the countryside, a parterre with a straight avenue down to the Octagon Pond, but other avenues westward into open ground. Vanburgh's Rotunda, first of the garden buildings, was sited where avenues met. After 1726 Cobham had William Kent and James Gibbs to design monuments, garden buildings (many called Temples!) and features which would evoke classical scenes as idealised in writings and, above all, paintings of the time. Kent sited them in a widespread area to the east, to make a series of pictures, so that each one gave different vistas of others and led the viewer to wander gently on. 'Capability' Brown was the gardener 1740-51, and helped with more natural layout of tree plantings, also use of water as pools and small lakes for reflections. Bridgeman's parterre was changed to a lawn. Cobham's nephew, Richard Grenville of Wotton Underwood, watched the creation of this landscape garden. When he succeeded to Stowe in 1751 as Earl Temple, he continued its development in the naturalistic style. The Octagon Pond was enlarged into the irregular Octagon Lake and Bridgeman's avenues were altered gradually to grassy glades. The garden, extending over 400 acres, was complete by 1779 when Temple died, after new north and south fronts had transformed his house into a splendid mansion. In 1847 the second Duke of Buckingham was bankrupt. The mansion in 1923 became Stowe School, and later had new school buildings near it. In 1989 the landscape gardens, retaining over 30 Georgian buildings, were given to the National Trust.

Milton Keynes new city is sited between the A5 and M1, on gently rising ground above the river Ouzel or Lovat. It covers 22,000 acres (8,900 ha.) and incorporates 13 ancient villages (kept intact) and the towns of Bletchley, Stony Stratford and Wolverton. Construction began late in 1970 from these towns towards the new city centre, industry and commerce being developed in step with the housing. It has a grid of main roads about a kilometre apart with a roundabout at junctions, making it a city of countless roundabouts. On wide grass verges many trees and shrubs soften the views and often hide all buildings. Cycle tracks, bridleways and footpaths are entirely separate. The areas of about a square kilometre between main roads have been developed either for commerce and industry or for housing. Workplaces are widespread to avoid traffic congestion. Housing is of all kinds and sizes, to rent and for sale, mostly of one design in one neighbourhood and none above three storeys. Each neighbourhood has its local centre. All houses are built to a better energy-efficient standard than nationally, but in Energy Park to an even higher standard and including business premises. Campbell Park is the central recreational one, there is a linear park along the river Ouzel including the Caldecotte and Willen lakes, another park along the Loughton Brook, and pieces of countryside are retained, such as Linford Wood. The city centre is more urban in character with taller buildings, but still an open layout with grass, trees and plenty of car parking. It uses different levels for roads. The shopping concourse has 140 shops under one roof; beside it are market stalls. The Food Centre, civic offices, library and banks are nearby. At the west end of the centre is the new station on the railway (London to Glasgow) and the bus station. Between them and the shops are offices, the hotel, and Central Business Exchange with Winter Garden. During construction archaeological finds have been fully recorded and some are displayed at Bradwell Abbey Field Centre. This is in a 17th century farmhouse near a 14th century chapel and cruck barn, both well restored as have been most old buildings here. The Open University has been based at Walton Hall since 1969. Milton Keynes is planned to have 250,000 citizens by the end of this century; it had two thirds of them by 1991.

17

EMBERTON.
In Emberton Park, the first country park in Britain and opened in 1965 by Bucks. C.C., its lakes being flooded gravel pits. BBONT have made a nature trail (orchids may be seen) and there is a mile of river bank. *June 1990*

LAVENDON. Near Lavendon Mill, floods of the Great Ouse looking towards Olney. *30 Jan. 1988*

RAVENSTONE. A remote village, Brickfield Farm hides 17C almshouses north of the church seen from an old pasture with ridge-and-furrow. *Feb. 1984*

18

BUCKINGHAMSHIRE

HANSLOPE.
By the Northants. boundary, the church steeple soars above the village on the crest of a low hill which has wide views to and from it. The tower is late 14C, but the spire was rebuilt in 1804 after being struck by lightning.   *March 1959*

NEWTON BLOSSOMVILLE.
A small farming village that is mostly built of stone. The church of c.1300 stands on the riverside, with a footbridge beyond it.   *Jan. 1974*

NEWTON BLOSSOMVILLE.
From the footbridge over the Great Ouse, late Georgian Cold Brayfield House shows beyond pastures. The next village downstream is Turvey, Beds.   *Nov. 1982*

GAYHURST.
Near the House is the classical
church, rebuilt from 1728 by the
Wright family.

Aug. 1965

GAYHURST. The interior of the Georgian church is almost unchanged with all its
original furnishings. The monument to the Lord Keeper Wright (died 1721) and his
son, George Wright was carved c.1730, and "is certainly not only one of the grandest
but also one of the most successful of its type in England" – Pevsner.   *March 1959*

20

CHICHELEY. International Baroque in style, Chicheley Hall was built of a glowing red brick with stone dressings, 1719-23 by Francis Smith of Warwick – a completely new and splendid house. With its garden, it is regularly open to the public. *April 1959*

GAYHURST. South front of the ornate House built of Northants. limestone and begun in 1597. Its park, which joins that of Tyringham, was worked upon by 'Capability' Brown c.1760 and Humphry Repton c.1790. *June 1959*

LATHBURY. The gateway to Tyringham designed by Soane and built c.1803 (restored in 1970s). "This is, in spite of its small scale, a monument of European importance" – Pevsner. *April 1959*

TYRINGHAM. The graceful bridge of 1797 by Sir John Soane spans the Great Ouse in the park. The house by Soane has been altered. *Aug. 1974*

LATHBURY. Looking north-east over fields in the Ouse valley towards Sherington – typical countryside with both arable and pasture.
1 Nov. 1970

SHERINGTON. The older part of the village has many houses and barns built of stone. It is dominated by the 13-16C church on a rise, the tower twice increased in height and a local landmark. There was rime on twigs of the large wych-elm.
Feb. 1972

MOULSOE.
A recently plashed or laid hedge (by Robert Sharpe) at Wood End Farm, its late Georgian house of red and yellow brick with a slated roof. This farm was established soon after Parliamentary enclosure.
April 1974

NORTH CRAWLEY.
Moat Farm at Little Crawley is 16C half-timber, much altered. It still has a bridge over the moat, here seen with English elms beyond it. *April 1959*

GAYHURST.
The London to Yorkshire motorway, later designated M1, during its construction.
June 1959

NEWPORT PAGNELL. The 1810 cast-iron Tickford Bridge – oldest iron bridge in Britain still bearing motor traffic – over the river Ouzel, called the Lovat here. The church is perhaps the most impressive town church in the county. *Feb. 1967*

NEWPORT PAGNELL. The various buildings in High Street, Nos. 68-70 with 16C chimneys, when it was a small market town. *June 1959*

MILTON KEYNES.
The tower mill at New Bradwell was built in 1815 of local limestone and worked until 1871. Restoration began in 1974 and is continuing. *July 1978*

NEWPORT PAGNELL. Just north of the town, water-meadows by the Great Ouse looking towards Lathbury, with an English elm (left). *28 Oct. 1961*

MILTON KEYNES.
Great Linford Manor House, a
noble early Georgian house of
stone (now offices) which faces
uphill to twin stables like large
lodges, with a vista between
them.   *19 April 1959*

MILTON KEYNES.
At Great Linford: the Prichard
almshouses with central
schoolhouse all c.1700, on the
drive to the church. They are
now workshops or offices, and
face mature trees and an old fish
pond by the canal. *19 April 1959*

MILTON KEYNES.
Houses at Solar Court, Great
Linford.   *9 April 1990*

MILTON KEYNES.
The Peace Pagoda, set up by Buddhist monks living in the city, stands above the north part of Willen Lake reserved for water fowl. The cannery and warehouses at Northfield are on the skyline. *14 July 1990*

MILTON KEYNES.
Willen church rebuilt 1679-80 of red brick and Portland stone to design of Robert Hooke, a close friend and collaborator of Wren. It stands at the end of an avenue of limes and was restored in 1970. *1 Feb. 1959*

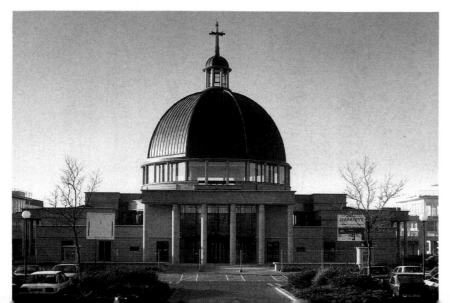

MILTON KEYNES.
The City Church of pale golden brick built in the centre during 1990-92, nearing completion. It is for use by five denominations. The Queen attended the opening service on 13th March 1992. *6 Jan. 1992*

MILTON KEYNES.
Windsurfers on the southern or sailing lake at Willen, one of the city's playgrounds. Another purpose of the lake is to prevent river floods due to run-off from roads.   *14 July 1990*

MILTON KEYNES.
The Point entertainments centre as a modern ziggurat seen from outside the central shopping concourse.   *16 April 1990*

MILTON KEYNES.
In the central shopping mall.
                9 April 1990

MILTON KEYNES. *The Swan* and an ancient elm in the village which has given its name to the new city.   *Feb. 1967*

BOW BRICKHILL. On the scarp of the greensand ridge bordering Bedfordshire, the brown sandstone tower of the 15C church, and part of the wide view over the clay plain on which the city of Milton Keynes is being built.
22 Aug. 1965

BUCKINGHAMSHIRE

THORNBOROUGH.
The oldest bridge in the county is a 14C one over the Claydon Brook. Nearby are two Roman burial mounds.   *April 1978*

THORNBOROUGH.
In the village, part of the irregular green which has a stream along it beyond the rails.   *April 1984*

THORNBOROUGH.
Built of stone, late 18C Mill House is on the Great Ouse.
          16 April 1990

BUCKINGHAM.
The top of Market Hill with belfry of
the much restored Chantry Chapel
(N.T.), which has a late Norman
doorway.   *Sept. 1970*

BUCKINGHAM. Down Market Hill with the Old Gaol of 1748 like a mock castle. The two Georgian houses (Nos. 11 and 12) have been replaced by a new store, and shop fronts added to most of the other houses.   *1 March 1959*

BUCKINGHAM. In Castle Street which has many Georgian buildings. The church was built on the castle site in 1777-81, but is mainly the work of Sir Gilbert Scott from 1862.   *April 1990*

BUCKINGHAM. The Georgian Town Hall (missing its gilded swan above the clock) and early Victorian *White Hart* face Market Square and the central junction of streets, with part of Georgian Trolly Hall along Castle Street.

April 1990

STOWE. The approach from the west crosses Oxford Bridge, built in 1761 over an artificial lake, and passes the two Boycott Pavilions of c.1728 named after a former hamlet. *Aug. 1958*

STOWE. The monumental south front 1771-75 designed by Robert Adam and given boldness by Thomas Pitt. It hides the 1676 house and makes a mansion grand enough for a duke. *April 1978*

STOWE.
North front of the Corinthian Arch designed in 1767 by Thomas Pitt, Lord Camelford, as an eye-catcher from the house and as the end of Stowe or Grand Avenue from Buckingham (avenue replanted recently). The arch contains two four-storeyed lodges.   *Aug. 1958*

STOWE. The Palladian Bridge of 1738 at the east end of the Octagon Lake.   *Aug. 1958*

STOWE.
On a hilltop east of the
park, Stowe Castle c.1746
is a large folly but has two
houses and barns inside it.
It has since become part
of a business park.
May 1959

STOWE. Near the mansion, the former village church has an unusual memorial, etched
glass showing Stowe or Grand Avenue and the two Lake Pavilions as seen from the
mansion.   *Aug. 1978*

MAIDS MORETON. The distinctive church completely rebuilt in mid 15C and unrestored. The churchyard has been over-tidied now. *March 1959*

MAIDS MORETON. Approaching the village on the north side of the Ouse valley. It has since become almost a suburb of Buckingham. *April 1978*

MARSH GIBBON. Near the church, the quite large Manor House of stone with a mid 16C two-storeyed bay window in its Jacobean east front. *March 1959*

HILLESDEN. The finest Perpendicular church in the county and one that inspired the young Gilbert Scott with his passion for Gothic architecture. Except for the tower, it was rebuilt from 1493 by an architect employed by the Abbot of Notley. The crowned turret linked with the house of the Dentons destroyed in the Civil War. *April 1984*

MIDDLE CLAYDON. The post office (closed 1981) in a Tudor-style house built in 1827 as a school for local boys. From 1877 for many years the schoolroom was used as a public library, rare in a 19C village.
21 June 1959

MIDDLE CLAYDON. Claydon House (N.T.), the remaining wing of a 1750-80 mansion to rival Stowe, added to his Jacobean house by the 2nd Earl Verney. Its sumptuous interior has elaborate decorations in three state rooms, and upstairs the even more lavish Gothic Room and fantastic carving in the rococo Chinese Bedroom.
21 June 1959

MIDDLE CLAYDON. From an upper window of Claydon House (N.T.), a view over the lake to open country and Steeple Claydon spire.
10 Aug. 1982

WINSLOW. The handsome Winslow Hall of 1700 by Sir Christopher Wren, built of locally-made red and vitreous bricks with stone dressings. *28 Feb. 1959*

WINSLOW. A small market town, this 16C half-timbered house with chevron brickwork is in a narrow street off the market square. *28 Feb. 1959*

BUCKINGHAMSHIRE

EAST CLAYDON.
A 16C timber-framed house near
the village pump, typical of older
houses in the villages centred on
Claydon House.   *21 June 1959*

SWANBOURNE.
A little village with many trees,
old cottages and houses like this
17C one, timber-framed with
brick infill.   *Sept. 1970*

SWANBOURNE.
Deveralls Farm has its house,
dated 1632, built of stone.
                    Oct. 1978

STEWKLEY.
The complete Norman
church without aisles was
built c.1150, a splendid
building that has a
beautiful west doorway.
The 16C pinnacles were
removed from the tower
in 1964.   *Feb. 1959*

STEWKLEY.
A timber-framed brick house with its
side wall of stone and plasterwork.
The large and straggling village is
festooned with overhead cables, as are
many others in the county.   *Sept. 1970*

SOULBURY.
A pair of terraced houses built in 1724
as Lovett's School and schoolhouse.
The large boulder in front is an erratic
of mountain limestone.   *Feb. 1959*

THE VALE OF AYLESBURY

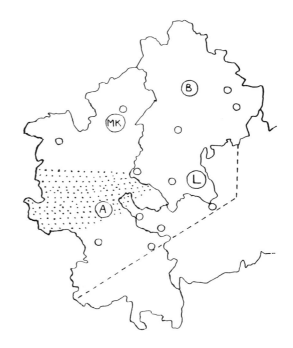

Aylesbury, the county town since the 16th century, has seen many changes recently, and its population has trebled in the last 40 years to over 50,000. The medieval trading centre clustered round the large church (severely restored by Sir George Gilbert Scott, 1850-69) on top of a low hill. The larger Market Square was needed in the 18th century. A printing works came here in 1867 (extended frequently until 1937) and a milk processing factory in 1870, followed by a slow increase in new houses – red brick and slated or tiled – making a dull urban spread to the east and south. In the 1960s London overspill was settled here, when the necessary new industrial and housing estates sprawled into the Vale, linked by a ring road. Much of the south side of the old town was demolished for the ring road, concrete and red brick car stacks, bus station, new shopping centre and market place, and the 1966 County Hall. From a two and three storey base a grey concrete tower of county offices rises eleven storeys, the upper floors with tiers of bay windows under pitched roofs. It is a brutal building, alien and out of scale especially with the defunct Market Square. Only as a landmark far across the Vale is it acceptable, but it may be respected later next century as a monument of the selfish 1960s. Humanity and much character has gone from the old town, where many houses are now offices; to the eye Georgian Temple Square and Church Street are the best of it.

Apart from expansion of Aylesbury this is still rural land, broad acres, about half of them arable, bounded by hedges with ashes and oaks; given variety by small isolated hills at Brill, Waddesdon, Quainton and Oving, with lower swellings from Chilton to Wing. Tiny streams drain into the river Thame, willows being common in wetter ground. Woods in the west near Wotton Underwood, Brill, Boarstall and Oakley may be remnants of Bern-wood, once a royal hunting forest. The many attractive villages have cottages of limestone where it could be dug out, and much local brick in warm hues, sometimes with timber framing. Interesting churches are the important Saxon one at Wing, 14th century Bierton and the 18th century interior of Lower Winchendon.

A splendid mansion, Wotton House was the country home of the Grenville family for 300 years. 'Capability' Brown was the gardener there in 1739, in George London's formal grounds with ornamental buildings and lakes, before going to Stowe. He naturalised them in 1742-46 and 1757-60. Other great houses are red brick and stone Chilton House about 1740 and Lower Winchendon House, the 15-16th century manor house made 'Gothic' 1790-1815. There are 19th century Rothschild mansions called Mentmore Towers, Ascott and Waddesdon Manor, all on hilltops with magnificent views.

AYLESBURY. At Broughton on south-east edge of the town, the Aylesbury branch canal of 1815 and many willows on the very flat Vale.   *April 1980*

LONG CRENDON. Summer floods of the river Thame cover a hay field near Notley Abbey.   *9 June 1985*

WING. In Ascott garden (N.T.): a topiary sundial, cedars and part of the view to the wooded ridge at Mentmore Towers and the distant Chilterns above Tring. *March 1978*

WING. At Ascott (N.T.) is a fascinating fountain with Venus in a shell drawn by sea-horses, designed by American sculptor Waldo Story. Golden-yew hedges and cedars are part of a winter garden for Leopold de Rothschild's hunting lodge, a 1606 half-timbered house enlarged in 1875 and extended c.1938. Rich furnishings and paintings can be viewed. *Aug. 1967*

MENTMORE. First of the Rothschild mansions, Mentmore Towers was built 1852-54 for Baron Meyer (his daughter married Lord Rosebery), to the design of Sir Joseph Paxton and G. H. Stokes inspired by Wollaton Hall, Notts. and of the same pale brown stone. From the low hilltop among trees it faces Aylesbury Vale. *June 1959*

WING. This church with fine 14C tower (see it from the west) looks medieval, but has a Saxon core including a crypt that may be late 7C. The Saxon polygonal apse, most intact one in England, has arched and triangular decorations and two blocked windows. It was built above the crypt in 10C. *Sept. 1970*

HULCOTT. Manor Farm has an intact moat on its land, east of the little church and houses by a lime-shaded green. *April 1980*

SLAPTON. Pleasure barges on the canal, looking to the distant hill at Ascott near Wing. In the opposite direction the view is to the line of the Chilterns. *Aug. 1978*

BUCKINGHAMSHIRE

AYLESBURY.
The bronze of defiant John Hampden
(1595-1643) in Market Square, with
former shops on a street corner. *July 1959*

AYLESBURY. Fine townscape in best of the few surviving old streets, Church Street – an 1840 Gothic front and a Georgian front (recent windows) on 16C houses, and a 17C timber-framed cottage with Georgian shop windows.
July 1959

WHITCHURCH. A little hill town with charm among the 15-19C houses lining its central streets, as here from the former market place down Market Hill. *March1982*

WHITCHURCH. Old houses in High Street seen over part of the motte of the 12C Bolebec's castle, extensive grassy earthworks giving a prospect over the vale to the Chilterns. *March 1982*

CRESLOW. On a hilltop surrounded by vast fields is Creslow Manor House, built c.1330 of stone. Its great hall was under the left roof, with solar wing (centre) and south-west corner tower; all much altered in 16-17C and recently. It is now a farmhouse. The village was depopulated on enclosure in 15C.
28 Feb. 1959

OVING. The view from Bunshill over pastures on slopes of these little limestone hills, to Pitchcott with Waddesdon in the far distance (see p.59). *7 Jan. 1991*

QUAINTON. The Winwood Almshouses built in 1687 of mellow red brick in pre-classical style, with Dutch gables on the two porches. They face the old rectory, now Brudenell House in a 2-acre garden (see p.58).   *Feb. 1959*

QUAINTON. Looking up the central green to part of the 15C market cross, Cross Farmhouse of 1723 (left) and the ruined tower mill, built of local bricks in 1830 and now being restored.   *Sept. 1970*

QUAINTON. The Buckinghamshire Railway Centre is at Quainton Road Station. Here a steam locomotive of 1898 hauls a train past carriages constructed in 1951 for Egyptian State Railways.   *15 Dec. 1990*

CHILTON. Chiltonpark Farm, with a late 16C and 18C house of different bricks, perched on a little hill – one of many around here – with trees at Waddesdon Manor on the farthest hilltop (see p.59).   *20 June 1971*

BRILL.
On top of an isolated hill with wide views, the village has 17C and Georgian houses of red bricks and tiles made at the pottery here from 12-19C. The clay was dug from pits all over the extensive common, seen from its south-west edge. The windmill dates from 1668 and worked until 1916.   *April 1984*

BOARSTALL.
An early 14C gatehouse to a moated manor house, Boarstall Tower (N.T.) was much altered in 17C when it became the manor house after the Civil War. This view is across the moat.   *April 1978*

CHEARSLEY. At the foot of the slope on which the village stands are 15-16C Lower Green Farmhouse and the 13C church with typical 15C tower of local limestone, above water meadows and willows by the river Thame. *March 1988*

ICKFORD. The river Thame, here the boundary with Oxfordshire, seen from Ickford bridge which dates from 1685. *April 1984*

LONG CRENDON. Just west of the church is the Court House (N.T.) put up in early 15C as a staple hall or wool store, but its upper floor (open to visitors) was used for the manorial courts.
June 1959

LONG CRENDON. A large village, formerly a market and wool-trade town, stands on a hill above the river Thame. The winding High Street leads to the church, passing *The Eight Bells* and 17C *Madges* seen on a spring morning.
April 1978

LONG CRENDON. The chapter house and refectory of Notley Abbey were built of stone in 13C. Here, in what is now a barn, is part of the ornamental arcading richly decorated with stiff-leaf on the wall of the refectory.   *9 June 1985*

LONG CRENDON. Notley Abbey (a private residence) is perhaps the best monastic building in the county – the ample lodging for the Augustinian abbot, 15C and c.1530.   *9 June 1985*

DINTON. This elaborate Norman south doorway has a tympanum carved with two monsters eating fruit of the Tree of Life, a Latin inscription and lintel showing St. Michael in combat with a dragon. *March 1959*

HADDENHAM. Much enlarged by housing estates, the rough green with a pond and Aylesbury ducks – reminder of former duck-rearing – retains the village air. The place is noted for walls of wichert, marl with water and chopped straw built up in layers on a stone base and rendered when dry. Garden walls were capped with thatch or tiles as here between the Manor Cottages. The tower of the 13C church is very fine. *June 1973*

OLNEY, Buckinghamshire. By the dredged river Ouse looking to the former mill house and to the fine early 14C church. Haws covered the bush (see p.16). *29 Nov. 1982*

TYRINGHAM, Buckinghamshire. Winter stillness by the Great Ouse in the park just after mist had cleared, facing towards Gayhurst from the bridge (see p.22). *14 Feb. 1984*

WOTTON UNDERWOOD, Buckinghamshire. Wotton House is colourful and has grandeur. Flanked by a pair of single-storey service pavilions and set behind a fine screen with gates, it makes a stately group facing east to Waddesdon Manor's tree-clad hill. Designed by John Keene and decorated by Thornhill, it was built 1704-14 for the Grenville family (see Stowe p.17, also p.43). *12 April 1988*

QUAINTON, Buckinghamshire. A village south of the rounded grassy Quainton Hill of limestone, that rises nearly 300 feet/95m. above it in open country. The church contains grand monuments of 16C and 17C (see p.50).
13 May 1987

WADDESDON, Buckinghamshire. Waddesdon Manor (N.T.), a grand Renaissance chateau by Destailleur, built 1875-80 of Bath stone for Baron Ferdinand de Rothschild, on bare Lodge Hill. At the same time garden-designer Lainé had long drives dug out and mature trees planted on the grassy slopes, to leave views to the Chilterns from this south-east or garden front. The mansion's interior and contents are equally fabulous.   *23 April 1987*

BERKHAMSTED, Hertfordshire. The freshness and timeless beauty of a Chiltern beechwood in springtime – tall beeches rising and spreading like fan-vaulting in a cathedral. The severe gale on 25th January 1990 shattered and uprooted many of these trees in Frithsden Beeches (Ashridge N.T.) (see p.87). *27 April 1984*

ELLESBOROUGH, Buckinghamshire. Autumn in Chisley Wood when most leaves had fallen from the beeches, looking to Beacon Hill and the Elizabethan house of *Chequers*. This part of the wood was devastated by the great gale in 1990 (see p.75). *23 Nov. 1983*

PITSTONE, Buckinghamshire. Fields among the downs – from Pitstone Hill (C.P.) this is over cornfields, nearly ready for harvest, to grassy Clipper Down (N.T.) and woods of Ashridge (see p.81).   *5 Sept. 1987*

MARSWORTH, Buckinghamshire. The abundance of flowers that can be found on the chalk in a nature reserve, College Lake Wildlife Reserve (BBONT). Here are several spikes of bee orchid, many blooms of common spotted orchid and yellow flowers of melilot (see p.80).   *4 July 1985*

ELLESBOROUGH Buckinghamshire. On Coombe Hill (N.T.) looking north to the Vale of Aylesbury over a profusion of flowers on the grazed west slope. The flowers include cream dropwort, red clover, musk thistle, yellow bedstraw and hawkbits (see p.75). *24 July 1985*

WHITWELL, Hertfordshire. Watercress being cut at Nine Springs watercress farm, a source of the river Mimram.   *26 March 1973*

KIMPTON, Hertfordshire. The English elm *(Ulmus procera)* seen in its golden glory, with the medieval church in the valley. The loss of so many great trees for several generations is grievous.   *11 Nov. 1973*

THE MID-CHILTERNS

This is the geographical area of higher land from Turville, Buckinghamshire north-east to the Gade valley north of Hemel Hempstead, Hertfordshire.

The irregular scarp of the chalk faces the Vale of Aylesbury and four valleys have been cut through the higher ground, which in its turn has been cut into by clusters of coombes to the south; all due to ice sheets and melt-water from them. The little south-flowing rivers are the Wye, Misbourne, Chess, Bulborne and Gade; all appreciably smaller now because of pumping for water supplies.

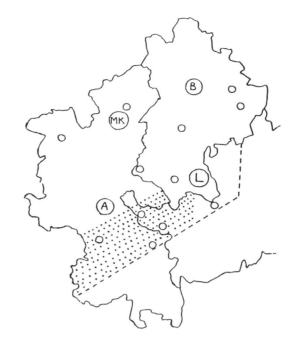

Soils are poor – chalky on the scarp, and clay-with-flints on the plateau – but well drained. Much of the land has been kept as woods, primarily oak and beech, the present dominance of beech due to 18-19th century planting. Furniture was originally made in the woods, later in workshops at Berkhamsted, Chesham, High Wycombe and elsewhere, but now as an industry mainly at High Wycombe. Pollarding and coppicing were practised to provide greater abundance of wood, loads of it once sold as fuel to London. Farming has always been mixed, formerly sheep on the downs; now more cattle are kept in pastures or corn is grown with fertilisers.

At West Wycombe is a Georgian planned landscape comparable with Stowe. This is due to Sir Francis Dashwood, a wealthy and talented eccentric, who modified his house to a Palladian mansion 1745-71, with frescoes by Borgnis. Formal grounds were laid out with buildings, a lake created and many trees planted to hide the village from the mansion. In this view to the north the old church (which stands in an iron age hillfort) of deserted Haveringdon crowned the steep hill. Dashwood had its nave rebuilt as a classical hall and the rest remodelled. The taller tower was topped by an eye-catcher, the famous golden ball. Also in 1763, just east of the church he erected the huge roofless hexagonal mausoleum, as an ornament seen from his home and coming from High Wycombe on the straight road he constructed in 1750-52. Chalk for the road's base came from the Caves, a long winding tunnel dug to relieve unemployment, with wider parts perhaps planned for his Hellfire Club, and entered from a sunken folly built of flint. Gradually the park was made less formal. Fine temples were devised by Revett, who added the east and west porticos to the mansion – the largest temple – and Robert Adam designed the stables. The delicacy of detail and decoration of these Georgian buildings are of a European tradition. Finally the grounds were simplified, with judicious tree-thinning or planting including those on Church Hill, from 1770-1803, partly as advised by Repton.

A lovely area of fields and woods crossed by footpaths is the farmed parkland of Great Hampden House and the Chequers Estate. The Forestry Commission has nature trails in Wendover Woods, but perhaps the best way to see this hill country is to walk the Ridgeway Path which, like the Icknield Way, follows the scarp from Avebury to Ivinghoe Beacon, and beyond.

At the north end of valleys through the hills, three small market towns now have extensive suburbs – Princes Risborough, Wendover and Tring, all on railways. Princes Risborough merges with Monks Risborough below Whiteleaf Cross, but has an interesting old centre, Church Street leading from the 1824 Market Hall to the late 17th century Manor House (National Trust). Wendover has 15-19th century buildings in the middle, through which the busy main road twists. Suburbs now meet Halton R.A.F. Station based on an 1884 Rothschild mansion, and from Coombe Hill suburbs seem to trail across the vale to Aylesbury. Tring has a bypass, but this cuts across the park of another Rothschild house (a school) below wooded hills. The town's buildings are dull except for the well-known mock-Tudor *Rose & Crown* of 1905.

Ashridge is an immense upland, where a 13th century monastery after the dissolution became a royal residence for Henry VIII's children. In 1604 it passed to the Egerton family, Earls and Dukes of Bridgewater. Wealth of the 3rd Duke of canal fame allowed the 7th Earl to rebuild his house, as a neo-Gothic palace of pale grey Totternhoe stone and designed by the Wyatts, 1808-21. Repton in 1813-18 helped to plan the confined gardens, in the vast park. The family's huge Ashridge estate was sold from 1923. The house is now Ashridge Management College, with new brick buildings on the west side. The restored gardens are open in summer, the chapel and hall occasionally. About 4,000 acres of the old Ashridge estate is owned by the National Trust, parts of the original commons of Ivinghoe and Pitstone in Buckinghamshire, and of Aldbury and Berkhamsted in Hertfordshire. There is downland, much woodland, commons and several farms. Original grazings on the commons have reverted to birch woods, often with bracken, and beeches have shaded out former grassy glades. However it is a lovely leafy area in which to roam. The great storm on 25th January 1990 blew down many trees, restoring former views above Duncombe and Aldbury on the west edge.

WEST WYCOMBE.
Among the downs, West Wycombe Park (N.T.) is an early 18C house remodelled c.1745-71. This double colonnade by John Donowell was added to its south front in 1754. On the hilltop is the gilded ball above the church tower and part of the huge hexagonal Dashwood mausoleum (see p.65). *July 1979*

WEST WYCOMBE.
The National Trust owns most of the village, which has some 15-16C houses among its many of 17-18C. The late 15C Church Loft is probably its best building.
July 1980

WEST WYCOMBE.
Down the steep Church Lane to Church Loft in High Street, backed by trees in the park.
July 1980

BRADENHAM. The post office is in a restored row of 18C cottages facing the green, a good example of use of flint with original local brick(right).   *July 1980*

BRADENHAM. The church, which has a Norman doorway, and the large red-brick classical Manor House c.1670 face the sloping green in this National Trust village, seen across the valley.   *Nov. 1982*

Near WEST WYCOMBE. Old farm buildings characteristic of the Chilterns – flint with brick dressings, weatherboarding and tiled roofs – at Slough Bottom Farm, with a wood mainly of beech above it. *July 1979*

FINGEST. Typical Chiltern countryside seen at its best from a pasture by Mousells Wood, over the little village and church with its mighty Norman tower, west to Cobstone Mill (a house) on Turville Hill, part of Turville village and a bridleway up to Turville Heath. *22 March 1990*

TURVILLE. On the somewhat overgrown common looking to Turville Heath House.
15 April 1981

TURVILLE. The village seen from a path on the lower slopes of Turville Hill. Turville Heath is beyond the hilltop beechwoods and nearly two miles away.
April 1980

Cherry blossom above a footpath near Turville Heath and, from the same path under another cherry tree, looking over fields and cherry blossom on the boundary with Oxfordshire. Northend is in the distance.   *15 April 1981*

TURVILLE. Near Northend is this view across the coombe to woods hiding Ibstone. Turville village is 1½ miles along the bottom to the right. *1 Nov. 1979*

IBSTONE. Close to the school on a sunny morning, looking east over mist lingering in a coombe. *8 March 1969*

MONKS RISBOROUGH.
The Ridgeway Path descending
eastwards from Whiteleaf Cross, through
a beechwood, to *The Plough* at Lower
Cadsden.   *April 1980*

RADNAGE. A scattered village, its delightful little church and former rectory are almost alone at north-west
end of a coombe below Bledlow Ridge.   *April 1979*

LACEY GREEN.
A smock mill erected at Chesham in
1650 and moved here in 1821. It has
been restored by the Chiltern Society
and faces across the valley westwards
to Bledlow Ridge.   *March 1990*

PRINCES RISBOROUGH.
Georgian and 17C brick houses in
Church Street seen from Market
Square. In contrast there is a R.C.
church of 1937-8 with a dome. Much
new housing for railway commuters
has spread the town to meet Monks
Risborough.   *June 1959*

PRINCES RISBOROUGH.
On the Ridgeway Path down
Whiteleaf Hill is this open view south-
west over the downland gap, to
wooded Bledlow Ridge ending at
Wain Hill 799 feet/244m. Near that
hill's northern foot, Bledlow village
stands above springs.   ▼ *March 1990*

ELLESBOROUGH.
On Beacon Hill 756 feet/230m.,
here is a small part of the
outspread Vale, with Aylesbury
(left). Buttercups were
flowering.   *13 June 1973*

ELLESBOROUGH.
The much restored church on its
little hill with the Vale of
Aylesury below it. The thatched
cottage-row has been extended
twice. The brick cottages are
almshouses of 1746.   *Aug. 1980*

ELLESBOROUGH.
Beacon Hill crowned with a
small bronze age barrow, from
the stile opposite the church.
                    Aug. 1982

BUCKINGHAMSHIRE

ELLESBOROUGH. From under beeches in Chisley Wood, the tree clump is on Beacon Hill and there is a glimpse of *Chequers*, the 16C brick mansion which is now the country residence of the Prime Minister (see p.61). *Nov. 1982*

ELLESBOROUGH. Near the same spot in Chisley Wood after the great westerly gale on 25 January 1990. Beech are shallow-rooted and should have oak and ash growing with them. *March 1990*

ELLESBOROUGH. Beacon Hill, the church and manor house on the edge of Aylesbury Vale seen from the Ridgeway Path on west side of Coombe Hill (N.T.), at 852 feet/260m. highest viewpoint in the Chilterns. The foreground slopes are grazed by sheep to keep their rich flora (see p.63). *Sept. 1990*

WESTON TURVILLE. On the south edge in Church End and facing the downs is the mid Georgian manor house, in gardens that are open occasionally in summer. There is a Norman motte and bailey in the grounds. *June 1973*

WENDOVER. Looking east down High Street to the 1842 Clock Tower and woods on Halton Hill. At the north end of a valley through the Chilterns, the little town has housing estates sprawling towards Halton and northwards. *4 April 1969*

BUCKINGHAMSHIRE

WENDOVER.
From the edge of a beechwood that covers the sides of a coombe, looking south-west towards The Hale, a house dated 1743, and the distant hills near Dunsmore. *April 1980*

CHOLESBURY.
Near the 1872 church are the banks and ditch of an iron age plateau fort that encloses 10 acres. Belgic pottery of the first century B.C. has been unearthed here. *Feb. 1986*

CHESHAM.
At source of the river Chess, a country town much enlarged to the north. In Church Street is the oldest house here, a partly 14C cross wing and hall; next to it a mid Georgian house with a carriage entrance. *April 1990*

BERKHAMSTED. Dignified early Victorian terraced houses in Chapel Street are typical of those in little streets between the main road (A41 or 'Akeman Street') and the canal. *Oct. 1990*

BERKHAMSTED. The Castle ruins (E.H.) with two moats, motte 45 feet high and fragmentary walls of flint, originally faced with stone and built c.1160-80. It was a royal castle in which the royal family lived, such as the Black Prince who held King John of France as prisoner. *8 April 1975*

HERTFORDSHIRE

BERKHAMSTED.
On Berkhamsted Common near Brickkiln Cottage: here and on the golf course, the poor soil of glacial deposits is acid enough for some heather (calluna) and gorse. *March 1980*

TRING.
To supply water to the canal's summit, Tring Reservoirs (NNR) were built 1802-39. Here are ducks, coot and seagulls at a hole in the ice on Startop's End Reservoir, looking north to Marsworth. Over 210 bird species including migrants have been recorded in the reserve. *2 Jan 1980*

TRING.
The second building of the Zoological Museum (by Huckvale 1906-8) built to contain the 2nd Baron Rothschild's collection, since 1937 part of the British Museum of Natural History. *Nov. 1975*

PITSTONE.
The cement works, with output of about one million tons per year, seen over a quarry into Lower Chalk near Marsworth, north of the road to Tring and west of the railway. *April 1971*

PITSTONE.
The same quarry was still being worked, but its nearer part is now College Lake Wildlife Reserve (BBONT). Many trees and bushes have been planted beyond the pools for ducks, in this view from a hide (see p.62). The cement works has since ceased production. (A lime works north of Ivinghoe Beacon has re-opened). *March 1990*

IVINGHOE.
The mid Georgian brewery house (YHA) and 16C Old Town Hall of timber and brick with 1840 gabled dormers, seen after a heavy shower. *2 April 1980*

PITSTONE. On Pitstone Hill (C.P.), looking east over tilled chalky soil to Clipper Down (N.T.) beyond its farm and to beechwoods of Ashridge (N.T.) (see p.62).   *11 Oct. 1973*

PITSTONE. From the Ridgeway Path on Pitstone Hill (C.P.), to the north are the Ivinghoe Hills (N.T.) with Incombe Hole (far right). Sheep graze here but hawthorns have to be cleared occasionally.   *11 Oct. 1973*

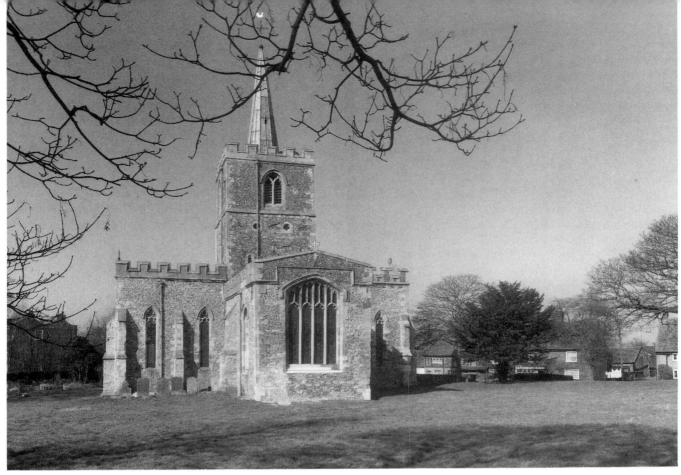

IVINGHOE. The church is a stately building, early 13C, its tower c.1330 with 15C top. *April 1980*

IVINGHOE. The lovely interior of the church has early 13C arcade capitals of Totternhoe stone carved with lively stiff-leaf. There are very similar ones at Pitstone, work of the same mason (see Eaton Bray, p.104).
Dec. 1958

PITSTONE. Here is an example of a Norman font of the Aylesbury type. The 13-15C church of flint and Totternhoe stone has been restored by the Redundant Churches Fund and is open occasionally.
Dec. 1958

IVINGHOE. Ivinghoe Beacon (N.T.) from the west showing chalk scar caused by too many feet (sward now restored). There are telegraph poles by the main road and a long stack is probably thatch over straw bales. The hillfort crowning the Beacon is one of the earliest in England, c.700 B.C.   *3 Sept. 1949*

IVINGHOE. On the Ivinghoe Hills (N.T.) above the lower end of Incombe Hole, this is the view north-west along the coombe to Ivinghoe church.   *Aug. 1982*

83

IVINGHOE. The view east from the Ivinghoe Hills to Dunstable and Whipsnade Downs, with cattle expecting more feed. The scarp in Whipsnade Wild Animal Park is kept clear of hawthorn scrub by wallabies! *28 Dec. 1968*

IVINGHOE. North to Ivinghoe Beacon (right) from National Trust car park farther up the hill road to Ashridge. The Icknield Way came through these hills in the gap left of and below the left summit. *28 Dec. 1968*

BUCKINGHAMSHIRE

EDLESBOROUGH.
This imposing church is on the west edge of the village (which is joined to Eaton Bray, Beds.), almost alone on an isolated hill in the vale, with expanses of corn to its west. The tower is 14C. Now restored by the Redundant Churches Fund, it has good woodwork inside. The church at Shillington, Beds. is sited likewise. *Aug. 1979*

EDLESBOROUGH.
A mid 16C tithe barn 180 feet long as it was at Church Farm. No longer a farm, the barn has been made the premises of a computer business. *June 1960*

EDLESBOROUGH.
Interior of the Tudor tithe barn with nine roof trusses and aisle bays. Note the thin brick infilling of the timber-framed walls. *June 1960*

ALDBURY.
In the church are the Whittingham of Pendley tomb and a fine stone screen, both of 1471 and brought from Ashridge in 1575. This is the heraldic wild or green man on the tomb.
Aug. 1976

ALDBURY. Founded in a forest clearing, the pretty little village keeps its triangular green with pond and stocks. Here it is seen from Tom's Hill on Aldbury Common, with fields rising to Aldbury Nowers which almost obscures the Vale of Aylesbury. Bushes now hide most of the village.
2 Nov. 1976

86

BERKHAMSTED. The last golden leaves on old beeches in Frithsden Beeches at Ashridge (N.T.) . The nearest tree was once pollarded (see p.60). *Nov. 1978*

ALDBURY. Mist in the damp woods of beech and oak on Aldbury Common. This wild woodland at Ashridge (N.T.) evokes the primeval forest. *Nov. 1979*

LITTLE GADDESDEN.
In a vast wooded park on the plateau is Ashridge, a romantic neo-Gothic mansion of Totternhoe stone by Wyatt 1808-13 and his nephew Wyatville 1814-21. It has a fan vaulted chapel with pinnacled tower and spire. Here we see only part of the north front which has Wyatville's entrance doorway and window, with the staircase tower behind. *April 1976*

◄ LITTLE GADDESDEN.
On the stairs in the 100-foot high staircase tower are eight statues by Westmacott, sculpted 1815-23, of founders and benefactors of the first English College of Bonhommes, here 1283 until the dissolution. This is a Bonhomme of Ashridge. *April 1976*

LITTLE GADDESDEN.
Slight mist and long shadows in the Golden Valley (N.T.), looking as intended when 'Capability' Brown landscaped this part of Ashridge Park in 1760-68. *15 Nov. 1970*
▼

HERTFORDSHIRE

GREAT GADDESDEN.
Water End lies by the tiny river
Gade with Gaddesden Place on
crest of the hill, the first house
designed by James Wyatt,
1768-73.   *3 May 1976*

GREAT GADDESDEN.
Across the Gade valley, a 16C
timber-framed house faces the
Moor (N.T.) at Water End seen
over the edge of the park of
Gaddesden Place. The bridge is
now slightly wider and some
trees have gone.   *5 May 1968*

HEMEL HEMPSTEAD.
A very fine and almost intact
Norman town church with
central tower, it is exceptional
for a rib vault c.1150 in the
chancel and a rare clerestory
c.1175 above the nave arcades.
The church with tall leaded spire
is on the east side of the Gade
valley, just below the most
attractive old High Street.
                     March 1976

THE NORTH CHILTERNS

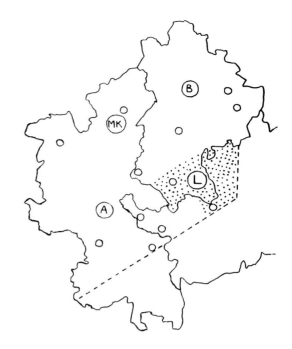

Here the chalk downs are broken by three narrow valleys with south-flowing rivers – the Ver (followed by Watling Street or A5), the Lea, and the Mimram in Lilley Bottom. There are also smaller side valleys. The summits become lower as one travels east, from 800 feet on Dunstable Downs to a little over 600 feet north-east of Luton at Warden and Galley Hills, and on Lilley Hoo at Telegraph Hill. North of these hills and the Lea valley the Lower Chalk forms a diminutive scarp from Totternhoe to Sundon, heightened by Middle Chalk above Sharpenhoe, Barton and Hexton, and capped by Upper Chalk above Pegsdon – the scarp's dominance increasing eastwards.

There is pleasant, little-known, countryside between the Lea valley and Hitchin, ridges and hollows with their rise and fall about 150 feet rather than the 300 feet in the mid Chilterns. Here are the typical Chiltern twisting lanes and many footpaths to hamlets; also scattered woods and copses in which oak predominates – not much beech was planted here on the clay-with-flints. Parkland is at Putteridge Bury (Luton College of Higher Education) and ancient oaks stand in a former deer-park at Kings Walden. However hedges are few and poor, as not needed for the arable made by merging the former little fields and pastures. Much loveliness has gone but it can still be found.

Hitchin was sited by springs of the north-flowing river Hiz that powered mills. It is a town now with about 32,000 residents, but its old centre keeps the original street plan, the market square and a number of good 15-19th century buildings. The church shows 15th century wealth from wool and tanning, with exceptionally fine woodwork of roofs and screens in its spacious interior.

Dunstable, now similar in size to Hitchin, was created from royal Houghton manor by Henry I who, in 1132, founded the Augustinian priory and gave the town to the canons. The Priory Church is the Norman nave of about 1150 of the original building, still magnificent though shorn of its former clerestory. It has been the parish church since 1392.

Luton is in the headwater valley of the river Lea. The valley is wide at its north-west end where the prehistoric Icknield Way crossed it. Early settlers used the river for watermills. Luton had at least two Saxon churches and at the Conquest was royal land. The present church was built 1131-37 to serve a great parish, comprising the present borough plus the parish of Hyde (separated in 1858). St. Mary's is one of the largest parish churches in England. Inside it is mostly early 14th and later 15th centuries – the periods of prosperity here – with a unique stone baptistry, transept chapels, twin-arched stone screen, two-storeyed sacristy and large 15th century windows. There was 16-18th century poverty, which ended in the 19th century when the straw hat industry centred more on Luton. Population increased 82 per cent during the 1840s to 10,648 in 1851, making it the largest town in England without navigable water or railway. Other industries came from 1871 and particularly from 1905 onwards. Growth of the town to the west and north was partly due to land sales by the Crawley family of Stockwood, their 1740 mansion demolished by the Corporation in 1964. Population of 61,342 in 1921 increased to 161,405 in 1971.

Local churches were built of the only materials to hand – flints bonded in mortar, and Totternhoe stone. This stone is a harder and slightly gritty layer found in the Lower Chalk. At Totternhoe this layer was near the surface and as much as 23 feet thick. From the 12th century tunnels were dug into the layer, blocks of stone hewn and hauled out. It was ideal for carving, work often done at the quarry. Externally it weathered badly, so in medieval times it was protected by regular limewashing. Stone from here was used in abbeys and palaces until early 19th century; now, for restorations, it is quarried from bottom of the lime works pit.

Bricks and tiles from local clay were made in very small amounts in medieval years. More were produced in 16-17th centuries, but in quantity during 18-19th centuries by farmers, landowners and builders in temporary local brickyards until superseded by the large Fletton brickworks early in this century. The Victorian terraced houses in Luton are mostly of 'Luton Greys', made in the town and at Caddington by about 30 brickyards; two in Stopsley and one in Caddington were in production until 1940, last of these little brickyards in the county. They used brickearth found in the clay-with-flints.

Today this is an area of great contrasts: the most splendid semi-natural landscape of the downs especially at Whipsnade, and above Totternhoe, Sharpenhoe, Barton and Pegsdon; 18th century created-beauty in the park of Luton Hoo, but the ugliness and depressing vulgarity of structures put up since 1966 in central Luton. The fumes and roar of traffic and jet aircraft assail the senses. Individuality has gone. The vastness of the Luton, Dunstable and Houghton Regis conurbation appals.

HARPENDEN. The Leys is a new shopping alley between High Street and shops in Leyton Road, designed by an architect. In its central court is displayed a painted relief representing sheep and the 'Baa-Lamb Trees' on Harpenden Common, a work of the local artist, Dora Barrett. *Aug. 1990*

KINGS WALDEN. Grazing is rare in this area now. Here is a pasture with mighty oaks, looking to two 16C timber-framed farmhouses on a frosty morning. The oak's trunk hides the pale grey roofs of many barns and cattle sheds. Large elms have gone but oaks are numerous. *23 Nov. 1983*

LILLEY. The village in its bottom and almost hidden by fine English elms, with Lilley Hoo on the skyline, seen from the hillside by the Luton to Hitchin road before it was made a dual carriageway. *July 1960*

PRESTON. A dell in Wain Wood, one of the secret meeting places where John Bunyan often preached when he had obtained temporary absence from his jailer. Much of the wood has had conifers planted in it. *Feb. 1978*

LILLEY. The little green abounding with nettles in the middle of this former estate village of the Sowerby family, who lived all 19C at Putteridge Bury, their crest a lion rampant as on the tiny cottage. *The Lilley Arms* is between the middle cottage and the tall elm. *July 1952*

HEXTON.
The view down the hill over fields set between woods, to part of the picturesque estate village and to Silsoe in Bedfordshire.
Nov. 1964

HEXTON.
The village pump erected in 1846 at the central crossroads. The first lamp above the original fingerboards was one that burnt paraffin.
Oct. 1977

PRESTON.
A pastoral at Offley Holes below woods on the little downs (see p.115).
May 1976

HITCHIN. The magnificent church shows 15C wealth of the town from wool and tanning. It is spacious, with chancel chapels, large windows, pinnacles, embattlements and two-storeyed porches – the south porch very grand. This east front is all built of stone. *March 1968*

HITCHIN. Early morning sunlight in Tilehouse Street, best street in the medieval centre of the town noted for variety of its attractive 15-19C buildings. This street was a main road when the photograph was taken, but is now a cul-de-sac. *June 1968*

BEDFORDSHIRE

LUTON.
In the Parish Church of St. Mary, the
unique baptistry and arch mouldings
of the west tower, both c.1330, show
how Totternhoe stone could be
carved. The baptistry has flamboyant
leaf carvings as crockets and finials on
its eight gables; originally it was
coloured and gilded (see p.116).
Aug. 1971

HYDE.
Someries Castle, not a fortress but a
prestigious house, demolished in 1742.
There remain ruins of the gatehouse
c.1448 and chapel c.1463 built of brick,
its earliest use in the county. Here part
of the south front of the gatehouse
shows the foot of newel stairs of brick
and use of moulded bricks, probably
made nearby. *March 1978*

HYDE.
A very distant view from near Copt
Hall of the east front of Luton Hoo, an
18-19C mansion remodelled by Mewès
in 1903. The park of 1500 acres (300 in
1623) was landscaped by 'Capability'
Brown from 1764. He made
undulating lawns, the sinuous double
lake (not visible here), and planted
many beeches and cedars of
Lebanon. *March 1981*

LUTON. The east end of Moat House, Biscot built c.1380 of flint with Totternhoe stone buttresses, its hall given a new roof c.1500 – the only medieval house left in the town. Chimneys were added later and c.1620 it was divided into two floors and smaller rooms. The moat is intact and was dug in 12C.   *13 Feb. 1957*

LUTON. Moulded purlins and principal rafters, embattled collar-beams and arched braces of the former hall roof, new c.1500; this is the only photograph of them before dereliction. My uncle was the farmer here for over 40 years. When derelict in 1963 these photographs induced Beds. C.C. to purchase the house from Luton borough, but Luton became a county borough in 1964. Eventually a local hotelier agreed to restore it as a restaurant.   *Flashlight, Nov. 1956*

The same roof timbers after restoration, above the dining room of *The Old Moat House*.   *Feb. 1976*

LUTON. The town centre in the Lea valley seen from the Church Cemetery, with the medieval church of St. Mary a jewel in the midst, but nearly lost although it is one of England's largest parish churches (see p.116). Cars in the industrial estate (right foreground) are on the site of the electricity works (see p.12).   *30 April 1983*

LUTON. Countryside in the borough: looking to Warden Hill over cornfields on Stopsley Common (see p.114). The man, who had been shooting pigeons, is returning from Common Farm (see p.15 – cameo of *Bedfordshire Magazine*).   *July 1964*

LUTON.
The municipal Airport (opened in 1938) when it was small – H. M. Customs and the reception building, with the nearly new control tower beyond them. The little aeroplane is a Chrisair and one man is carrying wheels of another light aircraft. There were 9,000 passengers in 1961, but 133,000 in 1963.
17 March 1962

LUTON.
Vauxhall Motors works – the more modern half of it – seen looking north on the footpath to Someries, above a car park. The present roundabout on Airport Way is at the road bend (right edge). *17 March 1962*

LUTON.
Capability Green, a new business park developed by Luton Hoo Estate on the north side of Airport Way. *18 Nov. 1990*

BEDFORDSHIRE

LUTON.
At Luton railway station: a steam
locomotive hauls a goods train, just
before steam locomotives were
scrapped. ▶

This was one of the new diesel-
powered passenger trains.
17 March 1962 ▼

DUNSTABLE.
The fascinating west front of the Priory church with a Norman portal c.1180, and a splendid doorway, arcading and two windows of 13C. The roof gable of the Priory would originally have been nearly as high as the parapet of the 15C tower (see p.116). *28 March 1965*

DUNSTABLE. In High Street North on a Saturday morning: the imposing and elegant Town Hall of 1880, using stone pillars of the late Georgian Town Hall burnt out in 1879. In 1964 Queensway Hall had taken its place, so it was demolished for new offices.
June 1960

DUNSTABLE.
The view north from Quadrant House, Church Street: showing Queensway Hall 1962-64 in the new civic centre, chimney of Waterlow's printing works and, at Houghton Regis, the cement works and church (right). The cement works stacks were demolished in 1976.
16 March 1968

HOUGHTON REGIS.
The huge quarry into Lower Chalk with greenish water on its floor, looking south-east to the cement works and Blow Downs beyond fields. The Manshead Archaeological Society of Dunstable recorded 3,000 years of life here on Puddlehill, as the sites of occupation were being destroyed by quarrying.
April 1951

HOUGHTON REGIS.
Tithe farmhouse beyond the yews and a Victorian house awaiting demolition for a shopping centre, a photograph taken on a frosty Sunday morning. The man probably had feed for poultry. The church has walls of stone and flint chequer and inside is a Norman font.
10 Jan. 1960

STUDHAM.
Chiltern countryside: freshly ploughed undulating fields on the east side of the Gade valley seen from under a beech *Nov. 1970*

WHIPSNADE.
In the Zoological (now Wild Animal) Park, a giraffe eyeing the visitors, with two baby giraffes in the distance. The zoo opened here in 1931. *18 June 1960*
◄

WHIPSNADE.
Part of the large irregularly-shaped green looking north-east, with *The Chequers* (right). The grass has been cut for hay, a tractor is towing bales of hay, while a class of children are being taught outdoors. Neighbouring Studham has a common of greater size which was originally more extensive.
▼ *3 July 1986*

DUNSTABLE.
Gliders of the London Gliding
Club above Dunstable Downs
looking north on a very clear
day. There is an open view from
here, the highest spot in the
county at 801 feet/244m. being in
the middle of a hedgeless
expanse of corn.   *2 March 1974*

EATON BRAY.
Sheep grazing on the downs
(Whipsnade Downs, N.T.) seen
from the road to Whipsnade,
with the line of a deeply sunken
way (left). This was the medieval
hill-grazing of the village out on
the lower ground to the north.
                    5 Sept. 1987

EATON BRAY.
On the scarp of Whipsnade
Downs (N.T.), sunken ways
cross one another. Looking to
Ivinghoe Beacon, this way winds
down a hollow up to 15 feet
deep. Not constructed, it is due
to countless feet of men and their
animals over many centuries,
and may be one of the tracks of
the ancient Icknield Way.
                    7 Aug. 1987

196
EATON BRAY.
In the church: part of the magnificent north arcade with shafted piers, stiff-leaf capitals and sumptuous mouldings, which is superb carving of Totternhoe stone c.1240. It was designed to have arches across the aisle. The south arcade of c.1220 is plainer but equally refined. The school of carvers for this work was based on the quarries at the next village. *Sept. 1990*

TOTTERNHOE. From the west, the lime works (left) and summit of Totternhoe Knolls which is the motte of a Norman castle commanding wide views. The lower west slopes are sites of digging for stone, humpy grassland (Local N.R.) with interesting flora that includes several species of orchid, also the great pignut which is rare outside the county. Much hill land to the east has been changed into cement. *Sept. 1974*

TOTTERNHOE. *The Cross Keys*, partly 15C, stands above orchards of 'Aylesbury prunes', a type of damson used as dye in the hat trade. As a boy in the mid 1930s my mother brought my younger brother and me on the bus from Luton, to climb the Knolls. We then had a boiled new-laid egg for tea in an orchard. *April 1950*

SUNDON. In Sundon Hills C.P. much of the land is pasture for sheep. Views from it range from Toddington on a hill to the west, past Harlington to Sharpenhoe below The Clappers, with glimpses of the greensand ridge farther away. *3 Aug. 1987*

SUNDON. Sharpenhoe Clappers (N.T.) and Markham Hills (centre) in the distance seen from Sundon Hill, over what is now Sundon Hills C.P., showing chalk of its old quarry. *1 Jan. 1967*

STREATLEY. The view seen from north edge of the National Trust car park. The Pulloxhill water tower does not show as the sun was not shining. Sharpenhoe is a hamlet of Streatley, the village on the hilltop to the south. *29 July 1990*

STREATLEY. The view as it was: down on Sharpenhoe, to Pulloxhill and the distant greensand ridge at Maulden (right) with King's Wood in Houghton Conquest (left centre), from the start of the path to Sharpenhoe Clappers (N.T.) with its mid 19C beech grove. Note the abundance of hedgerow elms. *26 Aug. 1956*

BEDFORDSHIRE

STREATLEY.
Ramblers near the south corner of the beech grove in winter when houses in Sharpenhoe, including Priory Farm (left), show clearly. This view is now lost because of a few large beeches on the scarp and big hawthorns by the path in the foreground.   *15 Dec. 1957*

STREATLEY.
Looking down on Sharpenhoe from the beech grove. The large red-brick house (left) replaced the row of 19C slated cottages, piebald houses were put on the farm site, extensions on back of the pub, dwellings on both sides of the whitened former chapel and huge barns at Bury Farm.
24 April 1990

STREATLEY.
In Sharpenhoe from the remains of an orchard: the chapel, the pub and the sign set up in Festival of Britain year stand below the 'Sharp Hill'. The 1990 view was from the edge of the beech grove on the right.
6 April 1957

STREATLEY. Near the south corner of the beech grove on Sharpenhoe Clappers (N.T.) looking north-west to Sharpenhoe, over the gault vale with many elms to Samshill and the very distant greensand ridge at Steppingley and Ampthill. Knapweed was profuse in the foreground (see p.113).
26 Aug. 1950

STREATLEY. The little spurs and coombes of the Sundon hills are distinct in evening sunlight from Sharpenhoe Clappers. The rise and fall here is only about half of that in the Buckinghamshire Chilterns, but there can be more beauty in the miniature.
5 May 1964

STREATLEY. From the south side of the beech grove on Sharpenhoe Clappers, this view to Barton church and Barton Hills shows the abundance of trees, mostly elms, in the south of the village. The woods on the skyline are at Hexton and a bit near Knocking Hoe beyond Pegsdon.   *24 Sept. 1974*

BARTON. Reverse of the previous view: Sharpenhoe Clappers over Leete Wood, a beech hanger, and the gault vale seen from Barton Hills with part of Plum Pudding (left), at the end of a long hard winter. Some elder scrub is in the foreground.   *2 March 1947*

BARTON. The hills around the head of Springs valley, with three people on Plum Pudden. The Springs are under white poplars at the foot of the sunlit slope (right). This view from just south of Leete Wood has been lost, because hawthorns grow on the viewpoint. *15 Nov. 1964*

BARTON. The lovely rounded humps and hollows carved in the chalk by ice sheets and the meltwater from them. These are the Barton Hills on the east side of Springs valley, now a N.N.R. for their plant-rich turf often grazed by sheep. The ash and alien conifers below Leete Wood are now taller. *22 Nov. 1977*

BEDFORDSHIRE

BARTON.
The Rectory, mainly timber-framed
Elizabethan, is on a moated site. Its
lovely garden is open occasionally in
summer. *26 Sept. 1974*

PULLOXHILL. ▲
From a meadow of East End Farm,
the view is over the 16C house of
former Hillfoot Farm and the gault
vale to the Barton Hills, with Springs
valley in the middle. Barton village
(before development) is almost totally
hidden by trees, many of them English
elms. *8 June 1958*

PULLOXHILL.
Gypsies with a Bow-top wagon and
English elms between Kitchen End
and *Speed The Plough*. *20 Sept. 1953*

111

PEGSDON:
a hamlet of SHILLINGTON.
The deep coombe, a dramatic feature
in the downs above Pegsdon, from the
path up its west rim. The banks across
its floor at the end are remains of a
wartime decoy, trenches in which
lights were turned on at night when
enemy bombers were near. Hawthorns
and briars now make thicker cover.
9 June 1968

▲
PEGSDON.
On a midsummer evening, over the
foot of the coombe north-east to lower
parts of these downs. Knocking Hoe
(N.N.R. – no access) is a darker little
hill (middle); beyond it on the highest
skyline is Knocking Knoll, what
remains of a neolithic barrow.
23 June 1966

◄
PEGSDON.
The summit of these grand downs is
Deacon Hill 566 feet/172m., which
gives a wide view to the west and
north. Here to the east, the Icknield
Way between the nearest double
hedge with trees is the county
boundary. Tingley Wood grows on
High Down of Pirton, Herts. (see
p.114). *2 Feb. 1983*

PEGSDON, Bedfordshire. Part of the imposing downland (now a Local N.R.) that rises above the hamlet, with Deacon Hill (left). Sheep and sometimes cattle, as here, graze the grassy slopes on which rows of lynchets show clearly. They were made by primitive ploughs turning the soil in one direction across the scarp, perhaps when population was high in the iron age. *11 Aug. 1974*

STREATLEY, Bedfordshire. Young leaves of beeches in evening sunshine on Sharpenhoe Clappers (N.T.) seen from the edge of the iron age promontory fort. The hillcrest path was small, but hawthorn scrub was encroaching. In Sharpenhoe the mid 19C row of six cottages had been demolished and one new white-walled house built, but the whitened farmhouse and barns still stood north of it. There were plenty of elms (see p.107 and 108). *6 May 1967*

PIRTON, Hertfordshire. The rich brown earth exposed when Wellbury Cottages Meadow on High Down (see p.112) was being ploughed. Many gulls and lapwings were after earthworms.   *26 Oct. 1983*

LUTON, Bedfordshire. Combine harvesters at work on Common Farm, Stopsley, the second machine emptying its grain bins into the trailer. Part of Warden Hill is on the left (see p.97).   *9 Aug. 1973*

HITCHIN, Hertfordshire. At Charlton, ridges for potatoes and lines of corn extend towards the little downs near Offley Holes (see p.93). A rider goes along the bridleway.   *9 Feb. 1984*

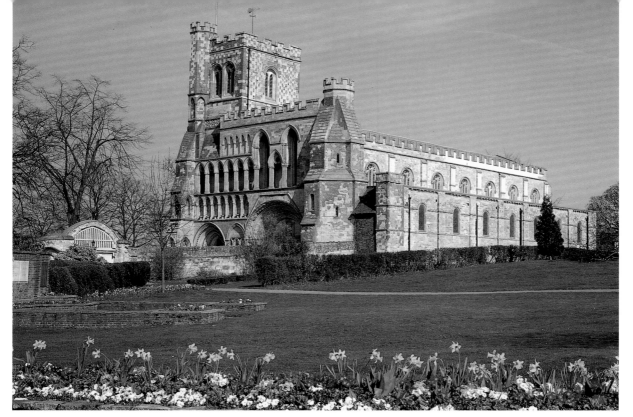

DUNSTABLE, Bedfordshire. The Priory church, a stunted remnant, but inside the massive Norman piers of the nave's seven bays reveal the magnificence of the original building. The impressive west front is mostly 13C work after the west towers fell in 1222 (see p.100). The 15C arches on the left are part of the gatehouse to the monastery. *17 March 1990*

LUTON, Bedfordshire. The Parish Church of St. Mary, a great medieval building of flint and Totternhoe stone, originally chequered only on the 14C and 15C tower but added to other walls during the 19C restoration. At that time the battlements were renewed, but changed to gables above the large 15C windows (see p.95 and p.97).
4 July 1983

SOUTHILL, Bedfordshire. A pair of 1797 estate cottages – timber-framed, plastered and thatched – in School Lane. Some of the ashes and top of the yew have since been removed (see p.142-3). *26 Nov. 1982*

PIRTON, Hertfordshire. South of the partly Norman church, buttercups and hawthorns flower profusely. This seems to have been the site of a fortified village-enclosure. Later it was the bailey of a 12C castle, the motte hidden by the tall elms. The water is in part of a moat. More recently the moat has been partially filled in, the grass sprayed with weedkillers and the large elms have died. *7 June 1969*

TURVEY. Bedfordshire. The Victorian Jacobean Rectory and typical 19C houses of limestone with yellow-brick chimneys in the attractive estate village. The Victorians restored the church and added the slated pyramid to its tower (see p.161). *1 Nov. 1970*

GREAT BARFORD, Bedfordshire. A scene of quiet and colourful beauty just above the narrow stone bridge, its west side timber-widening replaced with brick in 1874. This photograph was taken before Lombardy poplars and conifers hid the church and the river was dredged in 1975-6 for navigation. *14 Oct. 1972*

CARLTON, Bedfordshire. A man trundles his barrow along High Street on a sunny morning, a 17C stone chimney stack on *The Angel* showing behind him. The large stone and thatch house end-on to the street was the sturdy home of a 16C yeoman farmer. *The Fox* is out of sight (see p.161). *21 Oct. 1972*

FELMERSHAM, Bedfordshire. The splendid church of 1240, with 15C clerestory and top stage of its tower (see p.162), and the Old Rectory, all of local limestone that looks more golden in mellow sunlight. A United Counties bus waits for villagers going to shop in Bedford. *23 Oct. 1971*

OAKLEY, Bedfordshire. The contorted trunks of two ancient willow pollards stand in floods of the Great Ouse. In the distance, golden lichen covers the tiled roof of an old barn at College Farm (see p.160). *11 Jan. 1986*

HARROLD, Bedfordshire. There has been a bridge here since early 12C. This is the east elevation of the river bridge, which continues south over the causeway bridge (see p.164). The left arch is the oldest and the next arch a late medieval ironstone replacement. Stonework of the bridge and pinnacles on the church tower had just been restored. *13 March 1989*

GAULT AND GREENSAND

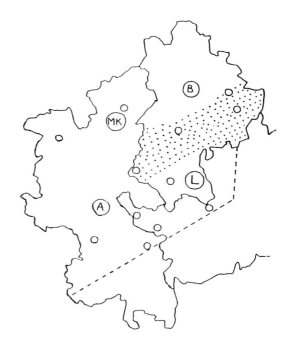

The thin sandy soils of the greensand ridge when first cleared of forest became grazing heaths, with gorse, heather and bracken; today mostly conifer plantations. Much sand was overlain by glacial boulder clay, thus left as woods. This land supported fewer people, so had remote places for Cistercian abbeys at (Old) Warden 1135 and Woburn 1145; also the Gilbertine Chicksands Priory 1150. In early 15th century a knight, Sir John Cornwall, built Ampthill Castle, later royal property where Katherine of Aragon lived pending divorce 1532-33. The sites of these buildings were used again for 16th century houses or 17-18th century mansions in parks, and there were new estates. Ampthill Park is now a public one where the Katherine Cross stands near the castle site, its 17-18th century mansion is private housing, and there are fine trees and views. To the north-east are the romantic ruins of 17th century Houghton House (English Heritage). Further east, Haynes Park a 1720 and 1790 mansion (Clarendon School) looks impressive from Church End of Haynes. Here or towards Clophill, distant views to the south are to the bold downs, Bunyan's 'Delectable Mountains', over the undulating gault vale, where lies the great park of Wrest with its stately mansion and landscape gardens (English Heritage). Down by the river Flitt, Chicksands Priory has 'Friends' restoring it, who also show to the public its many 18-19th century buildings with earlier vestiges.

To the north-east a lovely wooded and sandy area, with farms, is centred on the parks, with their lakes, of Southill and Old Warden. Both have delightful estate villages: Southill is scattered, thatched and plastered cottages or brick houses spread out on open flat land, but Old Warden is more showy and picturesque; made for the last Lord Ongley, from 1871 it was added to and well maintained by the Shuttleworths. It nestles in a valley among trees, its road winds on by the park and leads to Ickwell, with a maypole and cricket on the wide green. Northill has the church and boarded thatched cottages facing *The Crown* by a duck pond. Across the plain of the river Ivel, at Sandy with its pine-capped hills, are 18th century Hasells Hall (private apartments) and the Lodge (Royal Society for Protection of Birds), 1870 yellow brick Tudor by Clutton in a nature reserve.

The biggest influence on the county was the ducal one. The Russells were granted the Woburn monastic buildings in 1547, but no house was built until about 1630, which was in a small park. The present palatial Abbey is mainly 18th century, by Flitcroft and Holland. Much land was bought in the county and some in Buckinghamshire, the Bedford Estate's peak in 1877 of 37,186 acres, about a tenth of the county. Gabled Victorian houses usually of red brick and bearing the 'B', coronet and date can be found in many villages. The Bedford estate is now only a third of its peak size, but has farms and plantations mostly of conifers around the 3,000 acre park, which impresses by its vastness and now includes a Wild Animal Kingdom.

A good way to see this countryside is to follow in stages the 40 miles of the Greensand Ridge Walk, marked by muntjac deer emblems, from Leighton Linslade to Gamlingay, Cambridgeshire. It passes through the most interesting ground and the best viewpoints. Very little is on roads except in November to February, when a section through woods near Southill is closed and pleasant lanes are substituted. From the ridge one can see the low but sometimes quite large hills in the gault vale.

PIRTON, Hertfordshire.
On the Bedfordshire boundary, moated Pirton Grange is part of a late Tudor half-timbered courtyard house remodelled c.1700 and more recently. It is unusual in retaining its timber-framed gatehouse by the moat. The elms have gone now. *8 April 1976*

SHILLINGTON. From Upton End with 17C half-timbered New Farm, elms hide the village. Beyond the large church, a landmark on its hill, are woods above Hexton where Ravensburgh Castle, the finest contour hillfort in the Chilterns, is in the wood's edge next to the open Barton Hills. Playing-field floodlights now tower above the white pavilion (right). *March 1975*

SHILLINGTON. The hilltop church stands above 16-18C tiled or thatched roofs, with 19C slated houses of local yellow brick. Built of contrasting dark sandstone and limestone as large as the hill's crown would allow, the church's nave and chancel with aisles are as one, supported by eastern turrets and a 13C vaulted crypt. The west tower fell in 1701, its top replaced in plain Georgian red brick. *12 Aug. 1956*

MEPPERSHALL.
At this hilltop village, buttercups
and cow parsley did abound in
Church Meadow and the
churchyard. The church has a
Norman core but was heavily
restored in 1875-6. Facing it is
the Jacobean half-timbered
manor house, with ornamental
timbering as in the Welsh
Marches on its two larger
gables.   *1 June 1969*

SILSOE. The family of de Grey, Earls and a Duke of Kent of Wrest Park went to Flitton
church, to which their mausoleum of 17-19C monuments is attached (E.H.). They went along
this road lined by wych-elms at Wardhedges (pronounced Ware'edges), a landmark on a ridge.
Fall of boughs threatened felling, but Dutch elm disease sealed their fate.   *22 March 1958*

SILSOE. The de Grey family lived at Wrest for over 600 years. In 1834-39 Thomas Philip, Earl de Grey, first President of (R.) I.B.A., designed and built of Bath stone this French-style mansion with a lavish interior – first of its kind in England – here seen over the south parterre. Extensive formal landscape gardens (E.H.) were made 1706-40, modified by 'Capability' Brown 1758-60 when he worked on the park.   *23 June 1990*

SILSOE. The glory of these gardens is the Long Water with, at its far end from the mansion, this handsome banqueting pavilion 1709-11, a rare piece of English baroque designed by Thomas Archer. Inside is a ceiling painted by Hauduroy. The background gives a glimpse of the encircling canal that divides gardens from park.   *2 July 1977*

BEDFORDSHIRE

FLITTON.
On a market garden, Mr. A. Palmer of
Flitwick harrowing weeds between
rows of young celery. A horse was
used because a tractor would have run
over or put soil on the plants.
19 July 1958

FLITTON.
Three men with knives weeding
between young celery plants; their
hard work gained a good crop.
Unfortunately the celery leaves have
reproduced in the same tone as the dry
soil.   *19 July 1958*

FLITTON.
The same market garden, looking to
Maulden when it was a smaller village.
▼   *7 Sept. 1957*

FLITTON.
Changes that have taken place in Brook Lane – indigenous charm and wildness replaced by commercialism and overtidiness. The first cottage (No. 3) has been rebuilt to scale, retaining as much of the original as possible. Above all stands the mainly 15C church of local brown sandstone.

12 Sept. 1954

20 Sept. 1974

15 April 1990

19 June 1960

17 Feb. 1978

15 April 1990

TODDINGTON. Toddington Manor is a small part of an Elizabethan mansion with a round tower, much altered c.1833. It stands among fields below the hill, in lovely gardens made recently and open occasionally in summer.   *15 Aug. 1987*

TODDINGTON. The Square, site of the 16-17C market, is a large irregular green with many pleasing houses around it, the best, Wentworth House c.1700 of chequered brick (right). The old town hall had a cupola. Dominating all on the hilltop is the noble church, mainly 15C. A pony-drawn milk dray was still in use.   *26 Sept. 1954*

BEDFORDSHIRE

WESTONING.
The formerly pollarded Bunyan oak, one of his open-air pulpits, at Lower Samshill east of Harlington. John Bunyan was arrested when preaching here in 1660 and taken before the magistrate, Francis Wingate at Harlington Manor, before being committed to Bedford county jail. The dead stump had a young oak planted near it by Dr. David Bellamy in July 1988. *24 Feb. 1962*

MILTON BRYAN.
Mr. C. J. Creamer, of Church End, laying a hedge by the road from Toddington – work rarely seen in Bedfordshire now. Sir Joseph Paxton, the gardener and architect, began life at Milton Bryan. *18 April 1964*

TILSWORTH.
On low ground near the infant river Ouzel is the late 14C gatehouse to the moated manor house of the Chamberlain family. Built of sandstone, its roof was altered in 18C for use as a dovecote. The present farmhouse is not old. ▼ *2 Aug. 1974*

LEIGHTON BUZZARD.
The glory of this church, perhaps the finest in the county, is its late 13C central tower and great spire, seen here from the vicarage garden. The larger windows and flatter roofs are work of the 15C, when the long chancel was made collegiate. The chancel and steeple were devastated by fire in 1985. The church was re-consecrated in 1990. *29 March 1978*

LEIGHTON BUZZARD. The magnificent 15C Market Cross restored in 1852-3, early Georgian houses behind it of red and blue brick, and the Victorian *Cross Keys*, on a Sunday afternoon. There is now modern clutter of seats and signs here. *21 Feb. 1960*

HEATH AND REACH. Typical greensand heath, which has become a rarity, is in the park of Stockgrove House, now Stockgrove C.P. straddling the county boundary, where heather, gorse and bracken grow. There are also a large oakwood, pine plantation and marshes leading to a lake.
6 Sept. 1974

LEIGHTON LINSLADE. The canal was the county boundary between these two places until 1965. A commercial narrow boat is passing warehouses of a wharf, with the towpath bridge over the entry for barges. Only the bridge has survived redevelopment.
14 Aug. 1954

WOBURN.
The Chinese Dairy, built by Henry Holland in the 1790s, stands on the edge of Woburn Abbey gardens. These fine gardens were laid out by Humphry Repton in 1805-10, with great variety and to contrast with their surroundings.
14 April 1957

WOBURN. Woburn Abbey is a huge mansion, but seems small in the vastness of the park with herds of deer and great trees. Flitcroft's imposing west front of 1747 is seen over Basin Pond, reshaped by Repton during landscaping near the Abbey in 1805-10. The Duke of Bedford opened the Abbey and park to the public in 1955.   *25 Sept. 1955*

WOBURN.
The soaring interior of the hall church with stone vaults throughout, as decorated for Christmas. This building is considered the best Victorian one in the county.   *Dec. 1976*

WOBURN. The grand church designed by Clutton for the Duke of Bedford, with no expense spared, in late 12C French Gothic and built 1865-8 of Bath stone. Its spire was removed in 1890. This dominating building's size is shown by the car and lamppost.
18 April 1964

WOBURN. Beautiful and varied Georgian buildings face High Street and Bedford Street; more characteristic of a country town, they were built after a great fire in 1724 razed much of the village. Part of a main road, these streets are rarely without motor vehicles now.
5 Sept. 1954

WOBURN. Typical countryside of the greensand – walkers on a footpath and long shadows over ridges and hollows on Horsemoor Farm, west of the village.
27 Jan. 1957

HUSBORNE CRAWLEY. The church of local sandstone has blocks of many shades of glaucous green in its tower – a rare sight. Next to it is 16C Manor Farm of timber and brick, at top of the tiny green seen from a stackyard with a giant English elm. The thatched cottages were found on restoration to be cruck-built, perhaps 15C. *8 Sept. 1957*

HUSBORNE CRAWLEY. Lovely pastoral countryside with oaks and elms at Church End. *29 Aug. 1965*

ASPLEY GUISE.
The perfect south-east front of
Aspley House 1695, in lovely
grounds looked at from East
Street.   *22 Aug. 1965*

STEPPINGLEY.
A simple but charming 17C
timber-framed and thatched
cottage when it was the village
post office and shop.
                    20 Sept. 1953

MILLBROOK.
This timber-framed and
plastered cottage, with boarded
barn under the same roof, was
popular for pictures. Beyond it
are gabled Bedford estate houses
dated 1848, but elms hide the
hilltop church. A house of red
brick further from the road is
now on the cottage site.
                    20 Sept. 1953

HOUGHTON CONQUEST. Ruins of the west and south fronts of Houghton House (E.H.). Built in 1615, it was given splendour by classical features of stone central on three fronts c.1620, perhaps by Inigo Jones. In Bunyan's day it was an imposing landmark on the southern ridge from Bedford Vale and approached from How End, so traditionally Bunyan's 'Palace Beautiful' reached by climbing 'Hill Difficulty'.   *30 July 1966*

HOUGHTON CONQUEST. From Houghton House, this was the view over two ancient oaks of the park south-west along the greensand ridge, to chimneys of the Marston Valley Brickworks (now gone) and Cranfield hilltop beyond them.   *30 July 1966*

AMPTHILL. West from Woburn Street with a row of 17C thatched cottages backed by trees in Ampthill Park, before concrete lamp-standards were erected. The barn on corner of Claridge's Lane has been demolished, so the view is now open.   *5 May 1957*

AMPTHILL. In Church Street, 16C timber-frame and plaster contrasts with red brick Avenue House 1785, by John Wing of Bedford who enlarged it in 1819. This is down to Market Square and the crossroads, before the overhead lamps that so enraged the architect, Sir Albert Richardson. His former home, Avenue House, is still lovingly unchanged inside, its Georgian atmosphere intact.   *7 Sept. 1957*

BEDFORDSHIRE

MAULDEN.
On the south slopes of the greensand ridge, it was a very small village dependent on market gardens which come into its centre. The church was rebuilt in 1858-9 except for the 15C west tower. The timber-framed *George* sold J. W. Green's Luton ales then.   *27 June 1954*

AMPTHILL.
Looking from the greensand slope in Ampthill Park, with a glimpse of the Georgian mansion (private apartments). 'Capability' Brown landscaped the park 1771-2, making a winding west drive, mixed tree clumps, tree screens on the bounds, and the lake shown here with elms on the west boundary.   *6 April 1957*

AMPTHILL.
Near the same spot but at the top of the slope (two birches and a holly now on the left), replacement trees on the boundary are too small to show. Most of the brickworks' chimneys (except Stewartby) have gone from bare Marston Vale, seen under dramatic clouds of an approaching shower.
          15 April 1990

HAYNES.
A typical Georgian mansion, Haynes Park (now a school) has an imposing 1790 south front of stone, looked at from the road through Church End.
2 Oct. 1971

HAYNES.
Gypsies of Romany stock encamped by a lane in this widespread village with four Ends, all on undulations of the greensand. *March 1957*
◄

CLOPHILL.
Oaks on the high motte and earth ramparts of a bailey in the Norman knight Nigel d' Albini's castle at Cainhoe, headquarters of a powerful barony until mid 13C. Marshes protected the north-west side of the sandy hill, where the deserted village site lies. Following the Black Death, the present village grew north of the river Flitt. ▼ *8 Feb. 1970*

CHICKSANDS.
A Gilbertine priory was founded here c.1150. Its buildings are the core of this house: two 15C windows in the central cloister, from it the 13C doorway of the church, a 14C vaulted undercroft and massive timbers of 15C roofs. In 1813 Wyatt designed a new south and this east front retaining a 15C oriel. Home of the Osborne family 1578-1936, Dorothy wrote her letters here in 1652-4. *16 Aug. 1959*

SHEFFORD.
The place between 'sheep-fords' was a small country market town for 700 years, hence width of the High Street. It has 16-19C buildings, one re-fronted, a 16C former inn (left) over-restored, and shadows of R.C. St. Francis' Children's Society. Free of present traffic, litter and clutter, this was noon on a Sunday. *26 May 1957*

SHEFFORD.
19C houses and shops line North Bridge Street, with boot scrapers by doorways, the town pump, and a roadsweeper doing a good job. A replica of the pump is to be put on its site shortly. *5 Oct. 1958*

SOUTHILL. Georgian landowners and leaders of society displayed their wealth and taste in their houses and gardens. Samuel Whitbread, the brewer, bought mid 18C Southill in 1795, and his son engaged Henry Holland to remodel the house 1796-1800. This south front shows the use of widely-spaced pairs of columns, but also restraint that almost leads to severity. It is a peak of Holland's work in the most gracious decade of the age. *10 June 1990*

SOUTHILL. Seen through a hedge, a pasture in the middle of the village. Facing it are estate cottages dated 1796-7, timber-framed and plastered. Distant trees border the park which 'Capability' Brown landscaped in 1777, when he made its large lake. *30 Sept. 1982*

BEDFORDSHIRE

SOUTHILL.
Along the main street in this estate village are early 19C No. 64 (left) and 16C No. 32, both timber-framed and thatched cottages, but Nos. 33-35 are houses of yellow brick and tiled, 'S.W. 1855' on the porch (see p.117).　*2 Sept. 1982*

OLD WARDEN.
The small bush on the left is on the agger or causeway, about 30 feet wide, of a Roman road. It is seen from the present roadside, in an old marshy pasture called Claypits Field, east of the site of Warden Abbey. The hamlet nearby is called Warden Street. *29 Jan. 1974*

OLD WARDEN.
An estate village made fashionably picturesque in mid 19C by Robert, 3rd Lord Ongley. Cottages have gables, thatch or fishscale tiles, plastered walls washed cream or yellow, sometimes white timbering, neo-Tudor chimneys, a few fancy bargeboards and Gothic openings. All are well spaced in gardens below a wood. No. 16 is typical 'cottage orné'.　*20 Sept. 1974*

OLD WARDEN.
The Shuttleworth Collection of early flyable aircraft (also airship relics, veteran cars and motorcycles) was started in 1928 by Richard O. Shuttleworth. It is housed in hangars by the grass airfield. The earliest aeroplane is a 1909 Bleriot. Here is a 1923 DH53 Humming Bird and, beyond it, a 1940 DH Dominie 'Women of the Empire'.   *4 Dec. 1990*

OLD WARDEN.
On the north side of the park is the Swiss Garden (Beds. C.C. – restoration since 1976), a landscape garden with pools, hillocks, ornaments, winding paths and grass among clumps of bushes and fine trees. It was made 1820-25, probably by Peter F. Robinson, architect of Swiss Cottage in London and pupil of Henry Holland. It was well tended by the Shuttleworths, who built its Grotto in 1876. This is the Swiss Cottage.
26 March 1990

OLD WARDEN.
Warden Park, designed by Clutton and built of yellow brick in a Victorian Jacobean 1875-78, for Joseph Shuttleworth who bought the estate in 1871 from Robert, Lord Ongley. The clock tower was needed originally for the water supply. The house is now part of Shuttleworth Agricultural College.   *13 Dec. 1974*
▼

NORTHILL.
Ickwell, a pretty hamlet, stands round a spacious green with trees, a maypole, the former smithy, and tiled 17C manor cottages on the west side. Thomas Tompion (1639-1713), the master clock and watchmaker, was a son of the blacksmith. Here local children dance round the maypole.

9 May 1964

NORTHILL.
Nos. 35, 37 and 39 Thorncote Road were a charming group of cottages. They are now one whitened and thatched house, altered by speculators who are busy in this attractive village.

▼   *26 Oct. 1973*

DUNTON. On the east edge of the county, it is surrounded now by almost hedgeless prairie with few trees. However some land near the village is often used to grow flowers. The elms died in the 1970s. *26 April 1959*

POTTON. A country market town, very small until 1960, it has a market square lined by 18-19C buildings, Georgian red brick fronts on older houses but poor neo-Georgian on the west side. Just off the square, Sun Street keeps the atmosphere of the old town, Sun House, once an inn, being a medieval Wealden house with alterations.

16 Aug. 1959

146

EYEWORTH. The 15C spire was shattered by lightning on 20th September 1967, probably ball lightning and far beyond the capacity of the conductor. Some discharge had run over the rest of the building. The tower has since been made a gabled stump topped by a bell turret, and all the exterior restored.   *5 Nov. 1967*

EYEWORTH. Among trees on a low ridge, this handsome little 14C church had a spire – the only medieval one in the east of the county – added in 15C, as a landmark to rival the spires of Ashwell, Herts. and Steeple Morden, Cambs. to the south-east.
28 Aug. 1965

BIGGLESWADE. The character of High Street has been ruined. Why did the planners allow such a hideous frontage? The next building of yellow brick has lost the top of its chimney stacks and has new windows that are wrong. These were only the first changes!   *20 Sept. 1974*

BIGGLESWADE. An enlarged country market town, it is rather a mediocre place. Here are pleasingly varied buildings in High Street when it was part of the Great North Road, but was full of character, with the 1720 tower of the church beyond timber-framed houses at the bend. The side streets lead to extensive Market Square. *16 Aug. 1959*

THE OUSE VALLEY AND NORTH UPLANDS

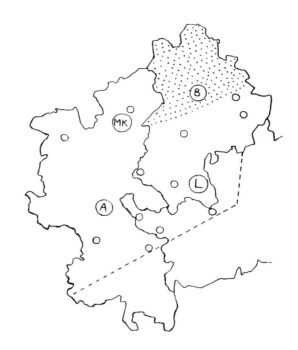

The dominant feature of this landscape is the Great Ouse which enters Bedfordshire from Buckinghamshire at Turvey, and flows through such tortuous meanders that its course is 28 miles to Bedford bridge, by road only about 8 miles from Turvey. Oolitic limestones have been exposed on the valley sides, the cream-grey stone formerly used for all buildings in the villages down to Bromham and Stagsden. A number of fine bridges of stone cross the river, as do blue brick viaducts of the railway south of Sharnbrook. Of nine stone road bridges: Turvey, Harrold, Bromham and Great Barford are partly medieval, Radwell is late 18th century and four others are early 19th century. The river still flows through open water-meadows (though some changed to arable), below steep slopes, past woods and by parks of country houses. In the past reeds for thatching and rushes for mats were harvested at Pavenham.

All the land is based on Oxford clay, the higher ground capped with boulder clay and rising about 200 feet above the river valley. To the south-west the hilltop plateau was wide enough for the aerodrome with Cranfield Institute of Technology; also north of Bedford for the Royal Aeronautics Establishment at Thurleigh, on a war-time airfield briefly considered in 1970 as a site for a third London airport. The northern uplands are broken by small valleys with streams. This undulating heavy land, now with few woods, formerly grew enough trees for the traditional timber-framed buildings, usually with plaster rendering colour-washed, and thatch for their steep roofs. Except in the north-west there is no stone, but stone was brought in for the imposing medieval churches, of which about half have stone spires.

In Marston Vale the Oxford clay is on the surface and has been brutally exploited by several huge Fletton brickworks with forests of chimneys, that came and have mostly gone this century leaving gigantic water-filled pits. One of them is now Stewartby Country Park, used for water sports as are neighbouring waters, but visited by gulls, water fowl and waders in winter when human activity is less. Along the Ouse and Ivel valleys, similar lakes occur where river gravels have been removed. Again some are used for water sports, but a few for natural history interest – birds, dragonflies and water plants – such as Harrold-Odell Country Park. The County planners hope to have many trees planted during the next few years to restore these devastated landscapes. They are being supported by the Countryside Commission for a 'community forest' in Marston Vale.

Bedford was founded by Saxons on river terraces where the Great Ouse could be forded. The river is now its chief asset: tree-lined walks behind County Hall and many willows along the Victorian Embankment, where the river has two channels crossed by foot bridges, with a meadow on the south bank. East of the third road bridge, Longholme Bridge built in 1976, is Newnham Leisure Centre; beyond it, Priory Country Park has lakes in old gravel pits. The town has lost much of its local character. Fine buildings remain, but they are overshadowed by concrete and glass towers or coffin-like blocks as in any commercial centre in the world. A new giant silvery-metal pyramid over a beach pool looks impressive against a winter sunset from Longholme Bridge, but it can disappear under a grey sky. People of all nationalities live here now, but there has been very good integration. The population, with Kempston and Goldington which are part of the town, has increased by half since 1951 to about 95,000.

RISELEY. High Barn Farm, south-west of the village, had this slogan against a threat of great change to the landscape. In Buckinghamshire, Wing was likewise threatened. The sand refers to Maplin Sands, Essex, another site considered in 1969-71 for London's third airport.   *23 Oct. 1971*

WILLINGTON.
Unusual traffic passing the huge dovecote which has two moulded stone doorways and nesting boxes for 1,400 birds, a valuable source of food for the large Tudor manorial establishment. The stone may have come from Newnham Priory, beside the river east of Bedford. The stepped gables probably derive from Flanders.   *26 March 1983*

WILLINGTON. John Gostwick bought the manor in 1529 and built its large house of brick. The remaining manorial buildings (N.T.) are the dovecote and 'the stable', the latter so used in 19C but it may be a late 15C or early 16C manor house. It was certainly a domestic building in Tudor years. The dovecote and rebuilt church are of 1530-41. People near the dovecote show the scale.   *23 Oct. 1982*

WILLINGTON.
In 'the stable', looking from the
window of the upper solar or
principal private room with a
fireplace in this Tudor house.
The window is of finely moulded
stone and was glazed with leaded
lights. The chimney stack has
been removed externally.
15 Sept. 1975

COPLE.
Opposite the church, many
gabled 17C timber-framed
cottages, one of them the post
office with its red-painted
telephone kiosk. *6 Sept. 1958*

RENHOLD.
At Salph End, Abbey Farm has
late 16C or early 17C half-
timbering. All the cows had their
horns. *22 July 1974*

CARDINGTON. A boarded and tiled haybarn on stone staddles standing by the moat at the entrance to extensive Manor Farm. The manor house, that became the farmhouse, was beyond many boarded or red brick barns. Now only the moat remains round the wooded site about 1½ miles south of the village. *26 May 1957*

CARDINGTON. The derelict manor house built of brick c.1540, with two stepped gables and a moulded chimney stack comparable with the contemporary one at Warden Abbey site (see p.10). It was the home of George Gascoigne (d.1577), poet, soldier and M.P. The white circle showed 'S.W.1769', date of a Whitbread restoration. *3 March 1957*

BEDFORDSHIRE

CARDINGTON.
On the flat vale, these two giant sheds 812 feet long and up to 180 feet high, built in 1927-8 for the R100 and R101 airships, are distinctive landmarks. One of the small airships produced in the 1980s is seen taking off.
14 April 1989

KEMPSTON.
The strange landscape created by the Fletton brickmaking industry at Kempston Hardwick in Marston Vale. A particular deposit of the Oxford clay is ideal for Flettons. Here machines have stripped off the unsuitable top layer, and a conveyor has dropped it as heaps in the worked out depths of the quarry.
Sept. 1968

CRANFIELD.
The first neo-Georgian building c.1937 of the Cranfield Institute of Technology, which began at Wharley End in 1946 as the College of Aeronautics, by the 1937 hilltop airfield on the county's west boundary. It is expanding, with many new buildings.
30 Aug. 1971

BEDFORD.
In St. Paul's Square: the east front of the town church is mainly 19C restoration of 15C work but impressive. Above the market stalls is John Howard, the penal reformer, a fine bronze by Alfred Gilbert on an Art Nouveau plinth. The market is now held on the site of the cattle market near the river. *2 April 1960*

BEDFORD. The centre of the county town: part of the Georgian bridge by John Wing, the red brick Shire Hall 1880, the 19C tower and spire of St. Paul's church, and the 1794 *Swan Hotel* by Holland at the start of the Embankment with its tree-shaded walks. *25 Nov. 1974*

BEDFORD. St. Peter's Green has a statue of John Bunyan preaching, with four scenes from *The Pilgrim's Progress* on the plinth, the work of Edgar Boehm. The exterior of St. Peter's is Victorian, with imitation Norman features on the tower which is actually Saxon. *28 Aug. 1974*

BEDFORD. Waiting for a bite: a quiet retreat by the river, with Prebend Street Bridge of cast iron 1883-4 – the second road bridge in the town – and part of County Hall 1968-9. The bridge is threatened with replacement because of heavy vehicles.
24 Oct. 1971

ELSTOW.
The church is the grand west end of the original nunnery church, the 15C east windows probably taken from the greater part of the abbey demolished in 1580. John Bunyan in his youth enjoyed ringing the bells in the detached 15C bell tower. Marston Moretaine has a similar detached tower. *9 Sept. 1977*

ELSTOW.
The village green, with a stone from a medieval cross, where John Bunyan often played tip-cat on a Sunday and once heard his 'voice from heaven'. He would still recognise the Tudor Moot Hall and the excellently restored half-timber of medieval houses along High Street. *17 Feb. 1978*

STAGSDEN.
Burdelys Manor was a small 'old-fashioned' farm at Bury End. Its ancient walls are of local limestone with brick chimneys, and within are a timber framework and a well. The pond is part of its 13C moat.
▼ *16 Aug. 1958*

KEMPSTON. The Great Ouse in flood where it is the boundary between Kempston and Biddenham (right). The nearest willow was once pollarded. *2 March 1958*

KEMPSTON. Church End is sited on the bank of the river, seen beneath thunder clouds. The church was founded by Judith, niece of the Conqueror, in 1100; it still has Norman arches in its tower and chancel. The village is now a suburb of Bedford but there are seven rural Ends. *12 Sept. 1954*

STEVINGTON. This was a site of early settlement by the Ouse. The church has a late Saxon tower (15C top) in which two windows and a tall narrow south doorway have been unblocked, opening into 14C aisles. The double-splayed south window has kept its original wooden frame. *Flashlight, Sept. 1967*

STEVINGTON. At the central crossroads of the lovely limestone village is the 14C market cross, restored with a 19C finial. It was one of Bunyan's preaching places. *18 Dec. 1985*

STEVINGTON. Cottages of stone and *The Royal George* in Silver Street, looking north to Church Street. *13 Nov. 1982*

STEVINGTON. Farm buildings of stone are rare in Bedfordshire. With a white willow beside them, this group at West End survives, but other stone barns here have been converted to housing. *13 Nov. 1982*

STEVINGTON. Alone in fields south-east of the village is the only remaining postmill in the county, seen over wheat with many trees in the valley. The mill dates from c.1770, had the tiled stone roundhouse added in 19C, was rebuilt in 1921 and worked until c.1936 using cloths on the sails. It was fully restored by Beds. C.C. for 1951 Festival of Britain. *27 June 1954*

OAKLEY.
Mute swans on the south channel of the river Ouse, looking to the church among trees on the north channel's bank (see p.120). This church has the only rood loft over a screen remaining in the county, with a painting on its coving; also a clock with one hand. *7 Feb. 1960*

PAVENHAM.
On The Moors are this once pollarded ash and the fine foliage of a short row of East Anglian elms (Ulmus minor), that have not been affected by the present Dutch elm disease. They are by the footpath that follows the river down to Stevington.
6 June 1975

PAVENHAM.
Another beautiful limestone village built mainly along a river terrace, but the church with a little broach spire is up a wooded hillside. This 16C house has its gable end to the street and pantiles on its outbuildings. Plaiters' Close for old people won a Civic Trust award in 1965. *20 April 1958*

BEDFORDSHIRE

TURVEY.
Elaborate ironwork c.1280 (and unrestored) by master smith, Thomas of Leighton, used on one of the original 13C south doors of the church (see p.118).

Sept. 1967

CARLTON.
On a summer's afternoon, High Street was like a gorge overhung by great trees and the tall gable ends of 16C houses of local stone. It was a small rural community then (see p.119).

▼ *27 June 1954*

FELMERSHAM.
The glorious west front of 1220-40 with its delicate detail is outstanding in a village, but this is the supreme 13C church in the county. The large window's tracery, flatter roofs and top stage of the tower are 15C changes, but they increase its grandeur. Inside, clustered piers of the tower contrast with a beautiful 15C screen (see p.119). *23 Oct. 1971*

ODELL. Village Farm built of local oolite, a fine three-storeyed 17C house with a broader and taller barn attached in line end-on to the road and facing the farmyard. The barn has orange pantiles. *24 Oct. 1980*

ODELL. From Little Odell looking to Chellington over a field of clover drying on tripods. Gravel has since been dug from under the field of ripening corn – site of the lake. Trees on the distant hill included elms.
4 Aug. 1957

ODELL. Across the Ouse valley to the redundant church (diocesan youth centre) of Chellington, a deserted village that moved down into Carlton. The lake in Harrold-Odell C.P. is good for waterfowl, with an artificial island created to encourage nesting.
24 Oct. 1980

HARROLD. Once a country market town, its market was revived in early 18C when this octagonal market-house was erected, a shelter for sellers of butter and lace. The market dwindled and ceased during 19C. Local limestone was used for 17-18C houses and the lock-up of 1824, but red brick later in 19C. *30 Oct. 1980*

HARROLD. Along the Ouse valley over floods in water-meadows seen from a path near Chellington church, showing part of the medieval 20-arch foot causeway and the causeway bridge. The river bridge (see p.120) is hidden among the trees. The 15C spire has thin flying buttresses to the tower pinnacles. *19 Jan. 1969*

PODINGTON.
On hilly land bordering Northants., a small village of stone with leafy hamlet of Hinwick that has two grand houses: Hinwick Hall, Tudor with an east front c.1700, and Hinwick House (see p.8). This row of 17C houses faces the church with a crocketed 14C spire. At the row's end is a late Victorian standpipe for water.
7 Aug. 1961

SOULDROP.
A tiny village set on the hill north of Sharnbrook, with views to the south. Its church has a 13C tower and broach spire – the oldest spire in the county. *The Bedford Arms* is timber-framed and end-on to the road, so perhaps late 16C, seen here when it was a plain 'local'.
4 Aug. 1957

SHARNBROOK.
A stone-built village varied by red brick houses, its High Street still has 17C limestone cottages, here with moss on old thatch. The late Victorian cast-iron standpipe, once usual in north Beds. villages, sent a jet of water from a lion's mouth into a pail when the knob on the side was turned; it was almost redundant.
29 May 1960

COLMWORTH.
This 15C steeple is typical of the medieval spires on these northern uplands and, like Keysoe, is a landmark of the plateau and of the long gentle rise from the east. Here it is in winter sunshine, from Manor Farm with a 17C dovecote. *4 Dec. 1990*

THURLEIGH. In undulating country the road twists through Scald End, with a fine English elm bursting into leaf. About a third of the trees here were elms. *12 May 1968*

Near COLMWORTH. Bushmead refectory in a dilapidated state, with tracery of a 16C window, and part of the Georgian mansion (demolished 1965) of the Gery family built on to an altered 15C kitchen wing of the priory. *13 Sept. 1958*

Near COLMWORTH. Of Bushmead Priory founded 1195, there remains this mid 13C refectory, restored 1978-84. The larger arch was originally a washing alcove in the cloister. The upper windows were inserted in 16C when the hall was made two storeys. Inside (E.H.) can be seen the hall's fine crown-post roof and some wall painting c.1310.
5 March 1985

KEYSOE. The most northerly cottage on the Kimbolton road, it stood alone and had a pretty garden with a plum tree. I called it the wee 'one-eyed' cottage. *12 Oct. 1958*

KEYSOE. The cottage while it was being restored. One can see that the rafters and purlins were merely coppiced wood. Just the original chimney stack and exterior proportions have been retained. *7 June 1986*

KEYSOE. 'The Cottage' as it is now. The garden wall is of brick to match those of the chimney. The garden of the next new house to the south has conifers looming above the cottage. *4 Dec. 1990*

BEDFORDSHIRE

SWINESHEAD.
The lovely street of this well-conserved village is much improved now electricity cables have been laid underground. Some houses are half-timber and colour washed, others timber-framed and plastered, with roofs of thatch or old tiles. The church is a beautiful 14C one, its lofty steeple 15C.   *5 April 1990.*

SWINESHEAD.
An English elm seen in its autumn glory. Good farm buildings show beyond it, also the 15C spire.   *23 Oct. 1971*

SWINESHEAD.
Moat Farm, the former rectory, is a charming 17C timber-framed house with tawny washed rendering, looked at from the edge of the tiny churchyard.
25 July 1978

INDEX OF NAMES AND SUBJECTS
(Illustrations in bold figures)

INDEX OF PLACES
(Illustrations in bold figures)

171

DEAN. The mainly 14C church with short spire has a perfect rural interior. Its low-pitched 15C roof has unusually rich carvings including an openwork frieze and angels, comparable with roofs in East Anglian churches.

23 Oct. 1971

Books Published by
THE BOOK CASTLE

JOURNEYS INTO HERTFORDSHIRE: Anthony Mackay.
Foreword by The Marquess of Salisbury, Hatfield House.
Nearly 200 superbly detailed ink drawings depict the towns, buildings and landscape of this still predominantly rural county.

JOURNEYS INTO BEDFORDSHIRE: Anthony Mackay.
Foreword by The Marquess of Tavistock, Woburn Abbey.
A lavish book of over 150 evocative ink drawings.

NORTH CHILTERNS CAMERA, 1863–1954: FROM THE THURSTON COLLECTION IN LUTON MUSEUM: edited by Stephen Bunker.
Rural landscapes, town views, studio pictures and unique royal portraits by the area's leading early photographer.

LEAFING THROUGH LITERATURE: WRITERS' LIVES IN HERTFORDSHIRE AND BEDFORDSHIRE: David Carroll.
Illustrated short biographies of many famous authors and their connections with these counties.

THROUGH VISITORS' EYES: A BEDFORDSHIRE ANTHOLOGY: edited by Simon Houfe.
Impressions of the county by famous visitors over the last four centuries, thematically arranged and illustrated with line drawings.

ECHOES: TALES and LEGENDS of BEDFORDSHIRE and HERTFORDSHIRE: Vic Lea.
Thirty compulsively retold historical incidents.

LOCAL WALKS: NORTH and MID-BEDFORDSHIRE: Vaughan Basham.
Twenty-five circular walks, each linked to an interesting topic.

LOCAL WALKS: SOUTH BEDFORDSHIRE and NORTH CHILTERNS: Vaughan Basham.
Twenty-seven thematic circular walks.

CHILTERN WALKS: BUCKINGHAMSHIRE: Nick Moon.
In association with the Chiltern Society, the first of a series of three guides to the whole Chilterns. Thirty circular walks.

CHILTERN WALKS: OXFORDSHIRE and WEST BUCKINGHAMSHIRE: Nick Moon.
In association with the Chiltern Society, the second book of thirty circular walks.

COUNTRY AIR: SUMMER and AUTUMN: Ron Wilson.
The Radio Northampton presenter looks month by month at the countryside's wildlife, customs and lore.

COUNTRY AIR: WINTER and SPRING: Ron Wilson.
The completion of this countryside companion pair, exquisitely illustrated.

SWANS IN MY KITCHEN: THE STORY of a SWAN SANCTUARY: Liz Dorer.
Foreword by Dr. Philip Burton.
Tales of her dedication to the survival of these beautiful birds through her sanctuary near Hemel Hempstead.

WHIPSNADE WILD ANIMAL PARK: 'MY AFRICA': Lucy Pendar.
Foreword by Andrew Forbes. Introduction by Gerald Durrell.
Inside story of sixty years of the Park's animals and people – full of anecdotes, photographs and drawings.

FARM OF MY CHILDHOOD, 1925–47: Mary Roberts.
An almost vanished lifestyle on a remote farm near Flitwick.

A LASTING IMPRESSION: Michael Dundrow.
An East End boy's wartime experiences as an evacuee on a Chilterns farm at Totternhoe.

EVA'S STORY: CHESHAM SINCE the TURN of the CENTURY: Eva Rance.
The ever-changing twentieth century, especially the early years at her parents' general stores, Tebby's, in the High Street.

DUNSTABLE DECADE: THE EIGHTIES – A collection of photographs: Pat Lovering.
A souvenir book of nearly 300 pictures of people and events in the 1980s.

DUNSTABLE IN DETAIL: Nigel Benson.
A hundred of the town's buildings and features, plus town trail map.

OLD DUNSTABLE: Bill Twaddle.
A new edition of this collection of early photographs.

BOURNE AND BRED: A DUNSTABLE BOYHOOD BETWEEN THE WARS: Colin Bourne.
An elegantly written, well-illustrated book capturing the spirit of the town over fifty years ago.

ROYAL HOUGHTON: Pat Lovering.
Illustrated history of Houghton Regis from earliest times to the present.

Specially for Children

ADVENTURE ON THE KNOLLS: A STORY OF IRON AGE BRITAIN: Michael Dundrow.
Excitement on Totternhoe Knolls as ten-year-old John finds himself back in those dangerous times, confronting Julius Caesar and his army.

THE RAVENS: ONE BOY AGAINST THE MIGHT OF ROME: James Dyer.
On the Barton hills and in the south-east of England as the men of the great fort of Ravensburgh (near Hexton) confront the invaders.

Further titles are in preparation

All the above are available via any bookshop, or from the publisher and bookseller

THE BOOK CASTLE
12 Church Street, Dunstable, Bedfordshire LU5 4RU.   Tel (0582) 605670

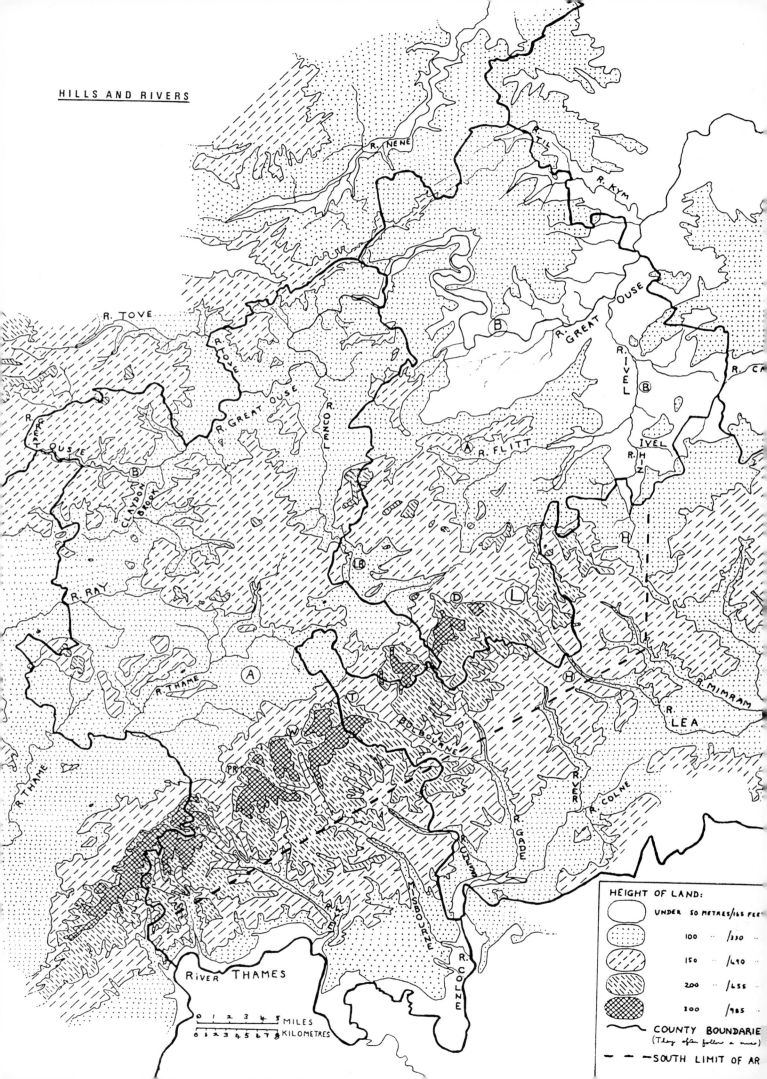

HILLS AND RIVERS

R. NENE

R. TIL

R. KYM

R. TOVE

R. OUSE

R. GREAT OUSE

R. OUZEL

R. GREAT OUSE

R. GREAT OUSE

R. RIVEL

R. CA

R. FLITT

R. IVEL

R. HIZ

CLAYDON BROOK

R. RAY

B

B

B

A

H

L

D

B

H

R. THAME

A

R. BULBOURNE

R. MIMRAM

LEA

R. THAME

T

W

PR

R. GADE

R. VER

R. COLNE

R. MISBOURNE

R. COLNE

RIVER THAMES

0 1 2 3 4 5 MILES
0 1 2 3 4 5 6 7 8 KILOMETRES

HEIGHT OF LAND:

UNDER 50 METRES/165 FEET

100 /330

150 /490

200 /655

300 /985

COUNTY BOUNDARIE
(They often follow a river)

— — — SOUTH LIMIT OF AR

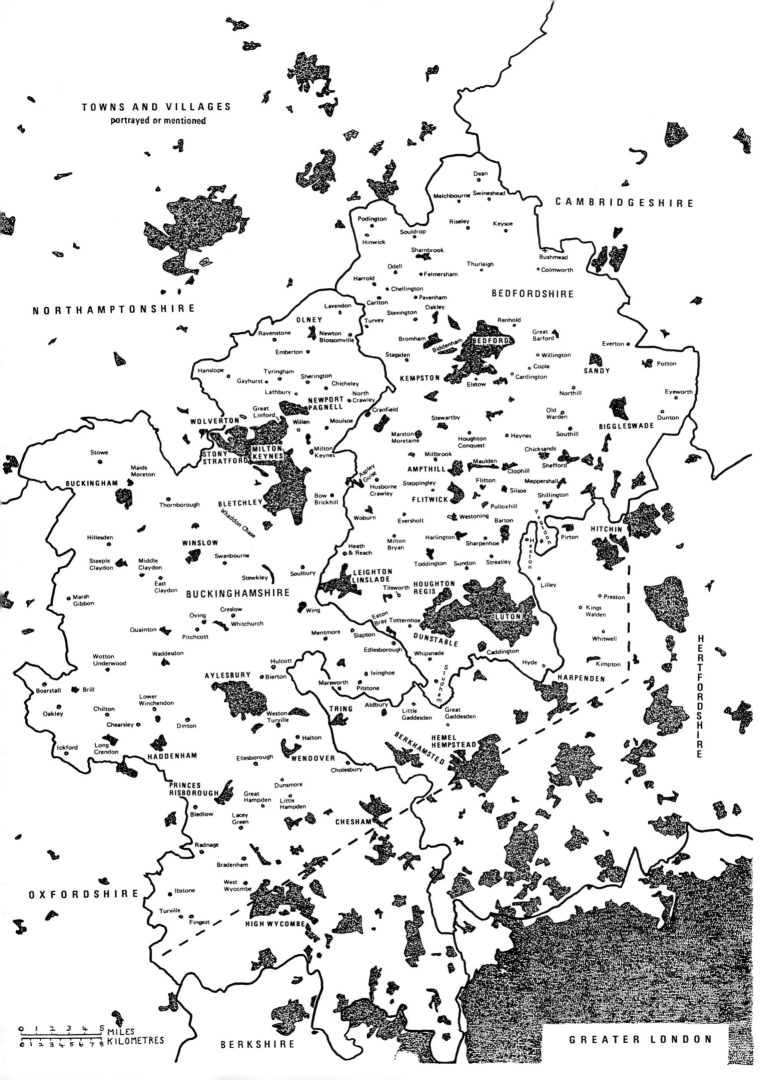

TOWNS AND VILLAGES
portrayed or mentioned

CAMBRIDGESHIRE

NORTHAMPTONSHIRE

Dean
Melchbourne Swineshead
Podington   Riseley   Keysoe
Hinwick   Souldrop
Sharnbrook   Bushmead
Odell   Felmersham   Thurleigh   Colmworth
Harrold   Chellington   BEDFORDSHIRE
Lavendon   Carlton   Pavenham
OLNEY   Stevington Oakley   Renhold   Great
Ravenstone   Newton   Turvey   Barford   Everton
Blossomville   Bromham Biddenham BEDFORD   Potton
Emberton   Stagsden   Willington   SANDY
Hanslope   Tyringham   Sherington   KEMPSTON Elstow Cardington Northill   Eyeworth
Gayhurst Lathbury Chicheley   Old   Dunton
NEWPORT North   Marston   Houghton   Haynes Warden
WOLVERTON Great PAGNELL Crawley Cranfield Stewartby Moretaine Conquest   Southill BIGGLESWADE
Linford Willen   Millbrook Maulden Chicksands
STONY MILTON Milton   AMPTHILL Flitton Clophill Shefford Meppershall
Stowe STRATFORD KEYNES Keynes Aspley Husborne Steppingley Silsoe Shillington
Maids   Guise Crawley FLITWICK Pulloxhill HITCHIN
Moreton Bow Woburn   Eversholt Westoning Barton Pirton
BUCKINGHAM BLETCHLEY Brickhill   Milton Harlington Sharpenhoe
Thornborough Whaddon Chase Heath Bryan   Streatley Lilley
Hillesden WINSLOW & Reach Toddington Sundon Preston
Steeple Middle Swanbourne   HOUGHTON Kings
Claydon Claydon Stewkley Soulbury LEIGHTON REGIS LUTON Walden
Marsh East BUCKINGHAMSHIRE LINSLADE Tilsworth DUNSTABLE Whitwell
Gibbon Claydon Wing Eaton Totternhoe Caddington Kimpton
Oving Creslow Mentmore Bray Edlesborough Whipsnade Hyde HARPENDEN
Quainton Whitchurch Slapton HERTFORDSHIRE
Pitchcott Ivinghoe Studham Great
Wotton Waddesdon AYLESBURY Hulcott Marsworth Gaddesden
Underwood Bierton Pitstone Little HEMEL
Boarstall Brill Lower Aldbury Gaddesden HEMPSTEAD
Oakley Chilton Winchendon Weston TRING BERKHAMSTED
Chearsley Dinton Turville Halton
Ickford Long HADDENHAM WENDOVER
Crendon Ellesborough Cholesbury
PRINCES Dunsmore
RISBOROUGH Great Little CHESHAM
Bledlow Hampden Hampden
Lacey
Green
Radnage
Bradenham
West
Ibstone Wycombe
OXFORDSHIRE
Turville
Fingest HIGH WYCOMBE
HERTFORDSHIRE

0 1 2 3 4 5 MILES
0 1 2 3 4 5 6 7 8 KILOMETRES

BERKSHIRE   GREATER LONDON